THE ALCHEMY LECTURE SERIES

The annual Alchemy Lecture is a collaboration between York University and Knopf Canada. Grounded in the idea of alchemy as a "form of speculative thought" and "a process of transformation and creation," it brings together distinguished thinkers from different disciplines and geographies to address the most pressing issues of our times. Each year, the Lecture takes the form of a live, multi-vocal public event presented by York University followed by a book published under the Alchemy imprimatur at Knopf Canada.

PREVIOUS LECTURES

Borders, Human Itineraries, and All Our Relation

Five Manifestos for the Beautiful World

The City of Our Dreaming

THE ALCHEMY LECTURE

Sound—at the Interregnum

THE ALCHEMY LECTURE

Sound—at the Interregnum

GLEN SEAN COULTHARD

CANISIA LUBRIN

MADELEINE THIEN

IMMANUEL WILKINS

Introduction by

CHRISTINA SHARPE

ALCHEMY

BY KNOPF CANADA

 Published in 2026 by Alchemy by Knopf Canada, a line of books within Alfred A. Knopf Canada, a division of Penguin Random House Canada Limited, Toronto.

Alchemy by Knopf Canada, an imprint of Penguin Random House Canada Limited
320 Front Street West, Suite 1400
Toronto, Ontario, M5V 3B6, Canada
penguinrandomhouse.ca

Library and Archives Canada Cataloguing in Publication

Title: Sound--at the interregnum / Glen Coulthard, Canisia Lubrin, Madeleine Thien and Immanuel Wilkins ; edited by Christina Sharpe.
Names: Coulthard, Glen Sean, 1974- author | Lubrin, Canisia, 1984- author | Thien, Madeleine, 1974- author | Wilkins, Immanuel, 1997- author | Sharpe, Christina Elizabeth, editor.
Series: Alchemy lecture series ; 4.
Description: Series statement: The alchemy lecture ; 4 | Fourth Alchemy Lecture held at York University, Toronto, on October 30, 2025. | Includes bibliographical references.
Identifiers: Canadiana (print) 20260138967 | Canadiana (ebook) 20260139165 | ISBN 9781039059610 (hardcover) | ISBN 9781039059627 (EPUB)
Subjects: LCSH: Sound—Social aspects. | LCSH: Sounds—Social aspects. | LCSH: Noise—Social aspects.
Classification: LCC QC225.7 .C68 2026 | DDC 306.4/5—dc23

Text design: Jennifer Griffiths
Cover design: Jennifer Griffiths
Typeset by: Daniella Zanchetta

Printed in Canada

10 9 8 7 6 5 4 3 2 1

CONTENTS

INTRODUCTION

In last year's Lecture, *The City of Our Dreaming*, the speakers collectively imagined the architectures and infrastructures that make possible, inevitable and irresistible gestures of freedom, modes of sustenance, and the necessity and pleasure of breaking bread together.

This fascism that we are currently living, this current backlash, is a brutal response to those architectures—a brutal response to all that we have worked for; we who believe that the earth is for everyone. The sound of George Floyd's murder on May 25, 2020, entered the world and drove millions of people into the streets; that sound resounded with injustices all over the world, and with people everywhere mobilizing anticapitalist, antifascist and anticolonial forces. All over the world people organized and stayed in the streets—demanding change and the end of brutality. Everywhere people were/are making other ways to live. As Dele Adeyemo writes, they "dared to block that infrastructure for profit with the infrastructure for another world."[1]

Five years on and all of the discredited white supremacists and their death-making ideologies and policies have returned to reinaugurate a murderous past that was not past. But they are not unchallenged. The sounds of refusal proliferate and do not respect militias and militarized borders. Sound travels when bodies, when people, cannot. Sound connects.

In addition to all of us braving the rain and gathered in person here, there are people joining us virtually tonight from Barbados, Belize, Brazil, Canada, China, France, Germany, Greece, Jamaica, Kenya, the Netherlands, Nigeria, Palestine, South Africa, Spain, Tobago, the UK, the US and Zambia.

A note, a word, a noise, a tap, a yell, a whistle, a shout, a song can move from one person to another, can join one person to another to another.

There are sounds of terrified arrival and departure.

The artist Dawoud Bey has made a film called *350,000* that imagines the sound of the 350,000 pairs of lungs and 350,000 pairs of feet of enslaved men, women, children, shackled and walking the three-mile path from the docks on the James River to the slave market in Richmond, Virginia.[2]

The sound of them shakes the earth.

Rebecca Belmore's conical sound sculptures *Wave Sound* resemble, on a massive scale, those first hearing aids called ear trumpets. Placed in four national parks in so-called Canada, "each sculpture amplifies the living sounds that are particular to the location" where it is installed.[3] Each sculpture asks that one practice embodied listening—a deep listening and feeling using one's entire body. *Wave Sound*, as Leanne Betasamosake Simpson has said, "amplifies the voices of water to cut through the noise of colonialism."

There are the sounds of extraction and greed. And there are the modes of listening, embodying and attending to what is around us that cut through those sounds.

In Gaza, there are the high-pitched sounds of drones, the loud explosions of bombs. One young person says, "sometimes it feels like [the explosions] are in time with his heartbeat" and he must hurry to find shelter before they fall on his head.

In "Breaking Bread Together" (in *The City of Our Dreaming*), Laleh Khalili writes that for Mahmoud Darwish, "as for many Palestinians now under siege in Gaza, the ritual of brewing the thick morning coffee was, is . . . a ritual of defiance and a way of connecting to the day, the news, the politics of things: [Darwish writes,] 'Coffee should not be drunk in a hurry. It is the sister of time, and should be sipped, slowly, slowly. Coffee is the sound of taste, a sound for the aroma.'"[4]

Sound is synesthetic.

The artist Lawrence Abu Hamdan worked "closely with the survivors [of Saydnaya—that notorious prison in Syria, that living grave] to establish a vocabulary for their memories."[5] Often blindfolded, isolated, unable to speak above whispers—the people who had been held there were earwitnesses to torture—those of them who survived, survived not only the assaults of the body but the acoustics of terror. Abu Hamdan's sound work attempts to "make audible those at the threshold of politics—the ghettoized, the political prisoner, the colonized, and the migrant."[6]

In *Wayward Lives, Beautiful Experiments*, Saidiya Hartman writes of the lives of young Black women in the first quarter of the twentieth century and the enormous risks they took in the face of total violence. "Nobody remembers the evening [Esther] and her friends raised hell on 132nd Street or turned out Edmond's Cellar or made such a beautiful noise during the riot that their screams and shouts were improvised music, so that even the tone-deaf journalists from the *New York Times* described the black noise of disorderly women as a jazz chorus."[7]

Sound is terror and witness and the improvisational noise of refusal.

Across the US, people are using whistles to warn other people that ICE is in or approaching the area. People are blowing whistles, honking, yelling at ICE to chase them away. This is a kind of protection in the midst of fascism.

Sound is sonic protection.

Writing about Paul Robeson, Shana Redmond says that "to hear his Voice during the 1950s was to hear his body performing under the conditions of McCarthyism."[8] After Robeson's passport was revoked and despite not needing one to cross from the US into Canada, he was prohibited from entering Canada. So, on May 18, 1952, Robeson gave an outdoor concert at the Peace Arch Park in Blaine, Washington, for people (almost 45,000 of them) who gathered on both sides of the US/Canadian border in order to hear him.

When Robeson's body could not move across borders, "the exception to his travel prohibition was sound."[9]

Sound carries.

The four speakers for tonight's Lecture, *Sound—at the Interregnum*, will carry us across time and space as each responds to my prompt:

> At this interregnum we meet oligarchs and fascists and manufactured crises of housing, ongoing genocides and displacements, extraordinary renditions, the takeover of universities and a deepening anti-intellectualism, the militarization of public space, the shrinking of the commons,

the use of sonic weapons (LRADs—Long Range Acoustic Devices), the complicit silences of mainstream media, and the refusal by those who have taken power to make a world in which everyone's needs are met. Their sounds of avarice and capital accumulation and immiseration do not enter the world uncontested. Sound is also key to life. There are the sounds of protest, of living and witness, of anthems and ululation, of chants and keening, noise of all kinds, blue notes, ghost notes, high notes—which also take us over as vibration, energy, atmosphere and breath itself.

What are the sounds you make? What are the sounds you want to make? What are the sounds you need to make? What are the sounds you need to leave to a world on the cusp of becoming something else?

The poet Don Mee Choi says, "If the language we create, reformulate, and recode can survive under the forces of language that occupies, militarizes, tortures, kills—then we made something happen."[10]

Tanya Tagaq sings, "They took our tongues / they tried to take our tongues / We lost our language / And we didn't."[11]

Tracy Chapman sings, "Don't you know they're talking about a revolution. . . . It sounds like a whisper." And it builds to a chorus: "Don't you know you better run run run run run."[12]

In the midst of genocides, in this time of tech billionaires and oligarchs, we gather here tonight, in person and virtually, in this interregnum, this in-between time, this possible time, and join these four speakers and each other in the spaces their sounds make.

—CHRISTINA SHARPE, Toronto, 2026

IMMANUEL WILKINS

"Improvisation isn't a refusal of the structure but the addition of new architectures—of care, resistance, indeterminacy and listening. It is the ongoing rehearsal of an alternative mode of existing, working together."

"Listen closely and you can hear another form of harm caused by the increase in mining development on our territory: the acoustic violence that accompanied the mine's operation."

GLEN SEAN COULTHARD

The Sounds of Extraction: Colonialism, Noisescapes and Auditory Resistance in Denendeh

GLEN SEAN COULTHARD

Introduction

When I was first invited by Christina Sharpe to participate in the 2025 Alchemy Lecture, my initial reaction was one of gratitude but also reluctance: Who the hell was I to speak about sound? Yet shortly thereafter, I traveled home to Denendeh—more specifically the homeland of my people, the Yellowknives Dene First Nation. I stayed at my cabin close to Dettah, a Yellowknives Dene community situated about thirty-five kilometers outside of Yellowknife, the capital city of the Northwest Territories, and one whose rapid growth from the 1930s to today has brought about significant change and upheaval for my people.

It was here that I began to sit with sound, and it was here that I first opened myself up to the invitation I was really being given—to approach my work from a new vantage point, one that would compel me to dig into the stories of my people in order to articulate more fully the material and affective experience of Dene resistance as it relates to noise and colonization.

Yellowknife, a community of now twenty-one thousand people, is situated on traditional harvesting grounds where the Yellowknives Dene have gathered, picked plants and berries, fished from the lakes and rivers, and hunted moose and caribou for thousands of years.[1] It was only following the discovery of gold and in the influx of white prospectors, missionaries, RCMP and bureaucrats that the sounds of these harvesting grounds were replaced by sounds of a different nature and entirely different scale—the noise of seismic blasting and underground mine expansion, bush planes, transport trucks, construction crews, and the everyday lives of more and more settlers. As John Sandlos and Arn Keeling write in their recent book, *The Price of Gold: Mining, Pollution, and Resistance in Yellowknife*, the scale of operations for hard rock mining involves intense and invasive activity compared to older techniques like panning. Loud, heavy equipment, bush generation of electrical power, mine working and ore processing facilities, housing and other infrastructures, workers and families.[2] All of this intrusively loud activity brought prospectors deeper into our territory for longer periods of time, so much so that it was rapidly becoming the new normal.

Writing and speaking about my home community is not something I often do. In the past, I have bristled at efforts to have me speak about my own personal connections to land and place. Over time, I have come to understand this bristling as a response to dominant settler narratives around indigeneity—the idea that to be Indigenous is to be not only rooted in but also shackled to a particular place. To be local. To have an identity and, in turn, intellectual contributions that are somehow delimited to a specific territory or homeland. Furthermore, to be Indigenous is to have stories, we are often told (even demanded)—a compulsion I have largely resisted in my academic work.

In other words, Indigenous Peoples have long been discursively and politically assigned to geographies of immobility, with indigeneity itself cast as one's ties to a specific community or territory. The discursive power of such delimitations for Indigenous Peoples has been realized time and again through the ongoing dispossession of our lands and the political marginalization of our communities, all in an effort to break our ties with the land and the expansiveness that this actually entails.

Over the past several years, I have been working on a new book about Dene political theory and activism in what I am calling the "long seventies"—the era of Indigenous political movements commonly referred to as Red Power. My desire has been to push back against such narratives, including within the academy itself, to articulate how Dene and other Indigenous activists theorized their anticolonial resistance in dialogue and exchange with other theorists and anticolonial movements—namely through deep engagements with the Black Power movements in the United States, Frantz Fanon, Mao Zedong, and the decolonization struggles of the Third World, radically reworked from within the frame of their own physical and cultural landscapes.

I have sought to demonstrate how, as Dene, our relational conception of land ties us to the political economy of those struggling against processes of land theft and occupation abroad. Theorizing this relational conception of land through the activism and organizing of George Manuel, Lee Maracle, Marie Smallface Marule, Gina Blondin, Phoebe Nahanni and many others makes clear that Indigenous relationships to land are anything but local and delimited; our people met, they traveled, they proliferated, and in doing so made sense not only of the ways things have been, but the way things may become. Land, from a Dene perspective, produces an expansive politics as opposed to one of constraint, and it's been my desire to illuminate the myriad ways in which Indigeneity and solidarity are born from inextinguishable relational geographies that surpass time and place.[3]

Until now, I have largely oriented this work around Dene resistance to oil and gas development in the Mackenzie Valley and uranium mining in the Sahtu, tracing the relations that resource extraction throughout Denendeh have materially connected us to the people of Palestine, Japan, South Africa and beyond. Yet I have only briefly touched upon the extractive violence on my own territory vis-à-vis the extraction of gold, as well as the significance that gold itself has had on the historical and contemporary anticolonial struggles of my own family and community.

Sitting at my cabin months ago now, sound suddenly became an invitation to examine the specific experiences of Yellowknives Dene with the same colonial apparatus of land theft and occupation, and to bring into sharp relief the enduring material and affective formations that sound continues to reveal. This has not been an easy task—the resentment that I have always channeled through my work on Indigenous political thought becomes even more visceral when I can turn to my family and community members and draw immediate connections between their own lived experiences and the cumulative violences of capital, colonialism and extraction.

My grandmother Marguerite passed away as I was writing this essay, and between the bookends of her incredible life, she witnessed the first settlers to Yellowknife and the permanent containment of her community—Dettah. She also experienced the noisy encroachment of an expanding settler community on lands she and her parents had traveled freely,

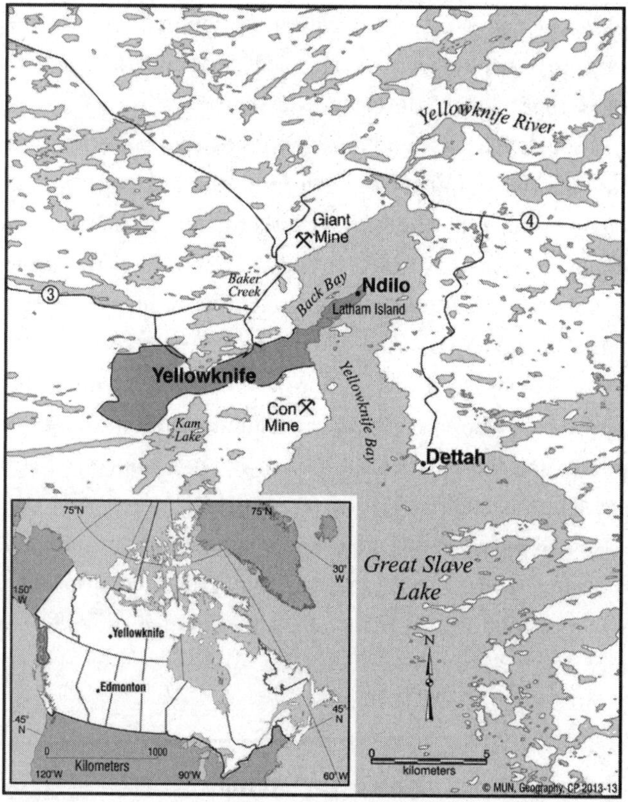

Credit: Charlie Conway, 2025

the start of the blasting at Giant Mine, the disappearance of the inconnu at the Yellowknife River, and the poisoning of her people and the land upon which they depended from the arsenic that poured, unchecked, into local waterways.[4] Yet her life, and the generations of family who recently gathered to honor her legacy, was also witness to parallel truths: the persistence of a Dene way of being and living even in the face of profound change, Dene uprising against a pipeline through the Mackenzie Valley, the tireless assertion of unextinguished rights to land, sovereignty and self-determination, and the silence that followed the closure of Giant Mine.

Though the profound noisescapes of gold have politically, economically and materially disrupted the relations that have sustained the Yellowknives Dene over generations, these sustaining relations nevertheless persist: relentlessly countering the noisescapes of colonialism through the auditory resistance of drumming, of gathering, of community *in spite of.* As Hopi scholar Trevor Reed writes, "music and sound are often tools or processes whose uses have consequences across a variety of political and social networks, human and non-human."[5] In this way, sound becomes a critical site for the expression of Dene resistance and renders legible a multitude of human and more-than-human forms of resistance that are often overlooked in scholarly efforts to theorize settler colonialism and resistance to it.

Noisy Newcomers

I want to examine the effects of Giant Mine on the Yellowknives Dene by paying particular attention to something I have often failed to consider in discussions of extraction and colonialism: noise. When people think of Giant Mine (or Con Mine, for that matter), they usually think of arsenic—the toxic by-product of gold extraction that still seeps into the land and water, poisoning game, fish, berries and, of course, our bodies. Arsenic contamination not only led to sickness and death in my community, but it facilitated a "profound alienation from a landscape that had, in effect, been colonized as a pollution sink for southern economic interests."[6] Between 1948 and 2004, Giant Mine released more than 237,000 tonnes of arsenic trioxide dust into the surrounding environment. Over that same time period, the local population grew from a few hundred to roughly nineteen thousand. It has often been said that if you could equally distribute all of the arsenic that saturates the land and water surrounding the mine site to every human being on Earth, you would have enough to kill the world's population several times over.

As I discuss in *Red Skin, White Masks*,[7] unlike many places in southern Canada, it wasn't until the inter- and postwar periods (depending on where in the North you're referring to) that several changes in the economic and political landscape of northern Canada began to overdetermine the character of colonial development there. Generally speaking, prior to the 1930s, Europeans were largely drawn to the North to find a water route to the Pacific Ocean via the Arctic, and then, later, by the desire to harvest directly, or indirectly through trade, the "marine and fur resources of the region."

Despite the increasing presence of Europeans in the North during these early decades of the twentieth century, Dene people were for the most part left as is: Our land-based knowledge and skill was central to the success of the economy. Although the Dene and Inuit way of life began to incorporate the use of new technologies (guns, traps, cooking utensils, etc.), the effect of such use was viewed as largely beneficial. Missionary presence in the North was also largely benign during this time; it wasn't until the postwar period that the church began to systematically intervene and disrupt our way of life.

However, the end of the Second World War brought about unprecedented and profound change. Soon after the war ended, Giant Mine officially opened, and production moved into full swing. The first gold brick was poured in Yellowknife on June 3, 1948. It was during this same time that the Dene found themselves having to increase their involvement in the wage economy of the emerging colonial society due to an increase in the cost of trade goods and a decrease in the price of furs following the world war. Subsequently, by the 1950s, many families had to supplement income derived from a hunting, trapping and fishing lifestyle with a combination of wage labor, welfare and family allowance. It was also during this time that the state began to enforce policies aimed at forcefully establishing settled Dene communities, arguing that this would better integrate adult workers into the new wage economy. The modern housing programs in the new settlements required the payment of rent as Dene became tenants on their own lands;[8] and the new rhythms of settlement life provided a context conducive to educating Native children in the skills required for attaining menial employment in an emerging industrial capitalist society. This so-called education increasingly took the institutional form of "residential schools," themselves used to encourage or coerce settlement so that parents could remain close to their children or as a requirement to access various forms of social welfare upon which Dene had little choice but to increasingly depend.[9] Essentially, changes in the political economy of northern development—where our knowledge and skills shifted from being central to the trade economy to being superfluous or even "in the way of development"—inaugurated a new strategy aimed at breaking the ties Dene people had with the land and the network of relationships and culture that the land fostered.

Yellowknife was at the epicenter of the profound and unprecedented change sweeping Denendeh. As a place, "Yellowknife" was first known to Europeans by the journal of Samuel Hearne in 1771; Hearne, when exploring the areas between Great Slave Lake and the Arctic Ocean for the Hudson's Bay Company, met Dene who used tools they had made from copper. Much later, in the 1890s, the next group of Europeans who made their way through our territory were prospectors en route to the Yukon goldfields, stopping to take samples at Yellowknife Bay that revealed the presence of gold and silver. However, the lure of the Klondike gold rush delayed any staking until the Canadian Geological Survey published findings of a mapping project in 1933.[10] Interest in the gold resources in and around Yellowknife increased in 1934 when the price of gold was raised by the US government from $20.67 to $35 an ounce.[11] The following year, however, the arrival of commercial aircraft (bush planes) made the area more accessible, and the gold boom took root. Prospectors arrived in greater numbers to hunt for precious metal along the northern shores of Great Slave Lake.

In my traditional territory in particular, gradual social and economic changes began to take hold following the "discovery" of gold around Yellowknife Bay in the 1930s,[12] although the full effects of this prospecting activity wouldn't take hold until the next decade. In the summer of 1935, C.J. "Johnny" Baker and H. Muir staked the original twenty-one "Giant" claims for Bear Exploration Company. The claims were on Great Slave Lake's Back Bay and along what is now known as the Ingraham Trail—all land within our traditional hunting and gathering grounds. According to oral history, a Yellowknives Dene Elder, Liza Crookedhand, discovered a "'shiny, heavy rock' while picking berries around [Baker] creek" and showed the rock to a prospector, who offered her "one or two stovepipes in exchange for the rock and information about its location."[13] Giant Gold Mines Ltd. was formed in 1937, but its operations came to a standstill with the advent of the Second World War. Gold was not a wartime priority, and the men who would have worked the mines were, in most cases, drafted. At the same time, Canada's wartime northern policy was much more focused on the mining of uranium and the establishment of military infrastructure in the Far North.[14] Nevertheless, the unequal exchange between Elder Liza Crookedhand and the prospectors produced the onslaught of white prospectors and miners that would eventually result in establishment of industrial hard rock gold mining and the opening of Giant Mine in 1949.

With the population boom that followed the gold mining industry establishing itself in and around the Yellowknife area came major disruptions to Yellowknives Dene harvesting grounds.[15] The political economy of the Yellowknives Dene is reliant on the extensive use of the land and animals—for food, medicine, clothing, spiritual sustenance and so on. Maintaining the relationships that sustain this mode of production means that certain areas must be left alone, at least where human settlement is concerned. As one community oral history explains:

> Elders discouraged families from living where animals, especially moose, would come because the animals would stop coming there. Otter and mink, for instance, leave a river

> where people camp on the banks; moose eventually leave an area where people stay. Thus, Weledeh Yellowknives families did not stay or build log homes in such places as the present day Giant Mine site.[16]

While the Yellowknives Dene have always been mindful of the impact of their actions on local ecosystems, prospectors and mining developments have not. Whites often overhunted sensitive areas, and the establishment of "camps, deforestation, blasting, and drilling" directly and negatively affected places that the community protected because of the significance they held for harvesting.[17]

In 1967, the federal government announced its plans to transfer the administrative center of the Northwest Territories from Ottawa to Yellowknife. Prior to this, Canada maintained direct control over northern political and economic development from Ottawa through the Department of Indian Affairs and Northern Development. After the transfer, the size and power of the newly formed Government of the Northwest Territories and its non-Native constituency increased dramatically. As the settler population continued to grow, the newcomers began to pressure the federal government to push even more northern economic projects to boost employment, mostly in the form of nonrenewable resource development. After all, the growing colonial society needed jobs, and the type of work the South had in mind for the North was resource extraction. If Giant Mine weren't already enough to contend with, we now had a burgeoning northern city and its noisy and invasive infrastructure on our territory.

This brings me to the topic of sound. Listen closely and you can hear another form of harm caused by the increase in mining development on our territory: the *acoustic violence* that accompanied the mine's operation. Before the mine, our territory was a quiet land of drum songs, stories and wind off the lake—a soundscape shaped by a Dene way of life on and in relation to land. Sound was not just background; it was part of how my people understood and related to the land. As our Elders often say, "The land speaks if you listen." Hunting, fishing and travel required an acoustic attunement to those subtle sounds: ice cracking, birds returning, moose calling, and the silence before the caribou arrive.

When Giant Mine began operations, that soundscape changed dramatically. The continuous roar of bush planes, blasting, drilling and crushing ore, and the constant hum of arsenic being released into the surroundings through smokestacks shattered the silence of the northern landscape. The mine ran twenty-four hours a day, seven days a week. The pounding of dynamite could be heard and felt for miles. It was as if one lived within a seismic zone, the blasts from the mine so powerful that their reverberations shook framed photographs hanging on walls and sent ripples through the bay that separated Dettah from the city of Yellowknife.

For Dene families living in nearby communities like Ndılǫ and Dettah, the sounds of the mine marked an intrusion—an acoustic occupation of our homeland. It wasn't just "noise" in a neutral sense; it was the sound of dispossession, the audible expression of colonial extraction. Scholars in sound studies help us understand that noise is never neutral nor merely technical—it's also political. It delineates whose voices matter and whose are silenced. The crushing machinery of Giant Mine drowned out the natural rhythms of the land. It replaced the sonic order of reciprocity with the mechanistic tempo of extraction for profit at any cost. It represented an entirely different way of relating to land.

This noise carried multiple effects.

First, it disrupted the ecological relations that the Dene depended on. Wildlife avoided the area surrounding the mine site; the vibrations drove caribou and moose from their traditional routes and scared fish from shallow bays. The very fish that Weledeh is named for disappeared from the river—their oily flesh, an important source of nutrition and sustenance, now out of reach. Hunting became harder; the land grew quieter in some ways and unbearably loud in others.

Second, the sound reinforced a psychological and social separation. The Yellowknives Dene were excluded from decision-making, and employment opportunities at the mine came with a profound experience of alienation and anti-Indigenous racism. Not only were we told to live with the noise, the dust and, later, the poison; the significance of these intrusions and their effects on our ways of life and our health were undermined by industry and government who were intent to reap the benefits of extraction at any cost—especially that of our lives and livelihoods. Noise became a reminder of our marginalization—a signal that the land's transformation was not being done *with* us, but *to* us.

Finally, the mine's noise continues in another form today, even after its closure. The government's "remediation project"—

which is estimated to cost Canadian taxpayers $4.38 billion, exceeding the profits and output of the mine over its duration—aims to freeze the arsenic underground and still requires heavy machinery, helicopters and drilling.[18] The Dene still hear the echoes of extraction—the "afterlife" of industrial sound and extractive colonialism. The mine may be silent at the surface, but the humming infrastructure of containment ensures that the sound of colonialism continues. It also ensures that my community will, in perpetuity, be locked into a precarious relationship of remedial care, as this infrastructure attempts to keep further environmental violence to our homeland at bay. Caitlynn Beckett writes that Yellowknives Dene "have been forced to accept that this underground threat could be there forever, returning to haunt them if containment technologies fail."[19]

Yet like the arsenic seeping into our earth and waterways, Dene bodies once again bear the disproportionate burden of ensuring this perpetual care—as Hall and Pryce write, "it is expected by both settler and First Nations government officials that Dene communities will constitute the majority of the remediation workforce engaged in remediation [at Giant Mine]."[20] The failed project of settler colonialism to break Dene ties with the land through extraction, settlement and residential schools now, ironically, ensures enduring Dene presence as caretakers of the disaster in perpetuity. And as Hall and Pryce further suggest, "while industry and government position Indigenous participation in remediation as a marker of extractive 'responsibility,' the constraints and inadequacies of remediation in meaningfully redressing the harms of extraction remain."[21] Returning to Beckett, while remediation implies a kind of endpoint—a realization of the healing of land—in actuality, this is perpetual care:

> While catastrophic events such as tailings dam failures make mining wastelands visible for brief moments of time, many of the chemical hazards produced through mining and controlled through remediation remain invisible and will "persist in a geological time frame that exceeds the timescale of the human species." For example, many hard rock mines result in acid rock drainage, which can require continual water treatment. In this sense, remediation plans should be framed as perpetual care plans rather than "clean-up" plans.[22]

Listening to Giant Mine through the lens of sound helps us perceive how colonial power operates not only materially but also acoustically. It's not only about what is seen—like tailings ponds or waste rock—but also about what is heard and felt. It is, as Alia Al-Saji has written, the "affective weight of colonization."[23] Or, as Rebecca Hall writes, it is "what it looks like to persevere through extractive relations."[24] The mine's sonic footprint altered how the Dene experienced our homeland, how we slept, hunted and prayed. It turned a place of resonance into one of reverberation—the kinds of reverberation that I felt as a child, riding my bike with my cousins through Dettah as the ground shook beneath us. Ironically, the environmental legacy of Giant Mine has compelled settlers in Yellowknife and beyond to finally grapple with the history of Yellowknife, forcing a coming to grips with the white frontier narrative that has been told time and again to represent the history of this place, a recognition that Yellowknife itself came at a great cost to my people and to the land upon which we depended and continue to depend.

There is another story that needs telling here: that is, the efforts on the part of the Yellowknives Dene First Nation to assert their sovereignty in the only language recognized by the settler state—a language that recognizes sovereignty through the state-sanctioned authority of modern land claims. Such politics of recognition formed the focal point of my analysis in *Red Skin, White Masks* and are indeed relevant here. In the years immediately preceding the establishment of Yellowknife as the political capital of the NWT, anticipation was building over the possibility of future petroleum discoveries off the northern shores of Canada and the United States. The excitement was justified; in 1968 a massive reservoir of oil and natural gas was discovered beneath Prudhoe Bay, Alaska. This resulted in an intensification of resource exploration in the Mackenzie Delta, the Arctic Islands and the Beaufort Sea. Subsequent oil and gas finds resulted in numerous proposals to transport these resources from the North to the South, including the use of tankers and pipelines. One such proposal was to build a pipeline corridor through the Mackenzie Valley, linking the oil-rich Mackenzie River delta with markets in the South. The outcry was swift from Inuvialuit and Dene whose homelands encompassed the pipeline pathway; they only needed to look to the gold mines in Yellowknife to see the significant impacts that resource extraction could have and with no Indigenous authority over land recognized.

In 1973, two monumental court decisions threw open the question of who owns and has jurisdiction over vast amounts of land claimed by Canada: *Calder et al. v. Attorney-General of British Columbia* (Supreme Court of Canada) and *Re Paulette and Registrar of Land Titles* (Supreme Court of the NWT). Both cases de facto challenged the sanctity of Crown sovereignty by asserting that the Indigenous claimants had never extinguished rights and title to their respective traditional territories (in BC, because the Nisga'a never signed a treaty, and in the NWT, because Treaties 8 and 11 fraudulently claimed that extinguishment was agreed to). In the NWT, this caused significant anxiety among the Canadian political and corporate elites vying for the Mackenzie Valley Pipeline. A federal royal commission was established in 1974 by then–Prime Minister Pierre Elliott Trudeau and his Minister of Indian Affairs and Northern Development, Jean Chrétien. Led by Justice Thomas Berger, the commission was tasked with evaluating the sociocultural, environmental and economic impacts of the proposed pipeline on the land and communities throughout the Mackenzie Valley region. Berger held community hearings across the NWT and Yukon from 1975 to 1976 to document the concerns of Indigenous Peoples and environmentalists. What became commonly known as "the Berger Inquiry" quickly revealed itself to be an incredibly strategic and significant channel through which northern Indigenous Peoples could assert their sovereignty at all scales. Dene organizing around the Indian Brotherhood of the NWT, which had been formed in 1969, was further galvanized through the community hearings process. For the first time in Canadian history, the Canadian Broadcasting Corporation reported by radio from Dene and Inuvialuit communities across the Mackenzie Valley region, transporting the voices and self-determination of northern Indigenous Peoples directly into the living rooms of southern Canadians.

Berger's report, issued in April 1977, concluded among other things that a pipeline from the Mackenzie Delta down the Mackenzie Valley to Alberta was feasible, but should proceed only after further study and after the settlement of Indigenous land claims. To allow for the settlement of land claims in the Mackenzie Valley corridor, Berger recommended a ten-year moratorium on construction, a term that the federal government accepted. Yet while Dene saw the moratorium as proof that their sovereignty could no longer be ignored, the federal government saw it as a means to achieve economic "certainty" through the extinguishment of Indigenous rights and title, creating a "safe" climate for extractive industry on Indigenous land.

The modern, or comprehensive, land claims process that resulted from the Mackenzie Valley Pipeline Inquiry took much longer than Berger's ten-year moratorium. In fact, the Akaitcho Process, which includes the Yellowknives Dene along with five other Akaitcho First Nations, has been ongoing since 1992—an endlessly frustrating series of negotiations with the Crown that has dragged on precisely because the city of Yellowknife sits within the claimant area. The state's vested interest in ensuring capital expansion and accumulation through land has slowed land claims negotiations in the Akaitcho region, while other claims elsewhere in Denendeh have been much quicker to finalize. This is not to say that our sovereignty is represented through the land claims process, however. In fact, as many Indigenous scholars assert, Indigenous sovereignty is produced and reproduced through ongoing, generative modes of relation—to one another and to land. While Dene lands and lifemaking may have been seen as sacrificial in the eyes of the state and of Giant Mine itself, the persistent and resistant *action* of Dene sovereignty over time serves as a reminder that our rights cannot be extinguished.

Drum Songs

Yellowknives Dene Drummers drum during a feeding the fire ceremony at the Giant Mine site. Photo: Emily Blake/Cabin Radio (2021)

Thus, amidst this noise, the Yellowknives Dene have continued to assert their own acoustic sovereignty. Through drum songs, ceremony and political speech, we continue to reclaim the right to define not only what sounds belong on our land, but how sound represents our relations to land. Our voices—raised in community meetings, public hearings, on the radio and through our music—counter the industrial drone that once functioned to silence us. In 1976, my grandfather and grandmother were present at the signing of the Dene Nation

Agreement in Principle, a monumental demonstration of Dene political voice, less than a decade after those same grandparents were granted the right to vote in a settler "democracy" that had long sought to extinguish their sovereignty and self-determination.

When we think about resistance to colonialism and resource extraction in the North or elsewhere, we often imagine blockades, petitions and political declarations. But for the Dene, resistance has also been expressed through sound—through the rhythmic, communal and deeply relational practice of drum songs.[25] These songs are not only cultural expressions but also acoustic acts of sovereignty. They challenge the colonial logics that render the land silent and extractable. They disrupt the timbre of state-sanctioned events with the reminder that we are here and always have been.[26]

Dene drum songs emerge from a way of life where the land is considered alive—where mountains, rivers, animals and spirits communicate with human beings through sound. In this worldview, to sing and drum is to listen to the land and to enter into reciprocal relation with it. When mining, blasting and industrial extraction drown out these sounds, the drum reasserts the land's voice. It interrupts the sonic violence of colonialism—the grinding noise of machinery, the explosions of dynamite, and the bureaucratic busywork of dispossession.

Extraction projects like the Giant Mine imposed a new soundscape on Dene territory: a noise of profit and pollution. The mine's ceaseless machinery didn't just alter the environment; it disrupted the acoustic relations that connect people to land, ancestors and spirits. Against this noise, drum songs work as counter-sonic forces. They reclaim the territory of sound as a space of Dene self-determination. Each beat of the drum insists that this land is not empty, not inert, not for the taking.

Drumming also enacts a politics of gathering: When Dene people drum together—at feasts, protests or ceremonies—they generate collective presence and memory. The drum unites voices across generations and communities, reminding listeners that resistance is not only about opposing extraction but also about sustaining life, family and community. It's a form of what some scholars call *acoustic* or *sonic sovereignty*: the power to control how a people's world is heard and understood. As Hopi scholar Trevor Reed writes, the power of sovereign song

> is an injunction to refrain from acting in a certain way within a particular place, backed by the authority of a network of powerful, long-term relations existing there. It confidently asserts jurisdiction, or a sovereign's general power to exercise authority over all persons and things within its territory. And yet, coming in the form of a song, some might mistake its true nature.[27]

At the official opening of the Giant Mine remediation project, the Yellowknives Dene Drummers opened the ceremonies in blessing the land—an acceptance of our responsibility to continue to care for the land, even when the damage done was not by our own hands, and a powerful assertion of the land's voice, a voice that has never been silenced. I could not help but be reminded of my colleague and friend, xwélmexw (Stó:lō/Skwah) scholar Dylan Robinson's reflection that Indigenous sovereignty isn't static or assumed: It is something we *do*.[28]

In this sense, Dene drum songs are not nostalgic survivals of a precolonial past; they are living, adaptive forms of political expression. Or, following Reed, a resonance of our political authority over our homelands.[29] They refuse the colonial demand that Indigenous sound be either folkloric or silent. The drum, instead, vibrates with what Kahnawà:ke Mohawk scholar Audra Simpson has termed *refusal*.[30] It asserts that Dene worlds persist despite extraction, that the land still listens, and that its people still sing back. Moreover, it demonstrates the (re)assertion of Indigenous sovereignty as perpetually relational, and as existing "within ongoing, generative relations, rather than being proscribed by a single, monolithic text or authority."[31]

Giant Mine's legacy is thus not only chemical but also sonic. It changed the way the land sounds and the way people hear. Paying attention to that noise has allowed me to hear colonialism differently. Listening carefully to the Yellowknives Dene teaches us that decolonization also requires relistening—to the land, to the rhythm of generative relations, and to the sounds of resistance that continue to rise from us.

Conclusion

In accepting the invitation to write this piece, I was called to consider sound as both a marker of colonial ecological violence, as Lauren Knight suggests,[32] as well as an assertion of Dene sovereignty and indeed Dene futures. This task has been challenging for me, and I wrestled with writing this piece more than I have with any other. Bringing the political and the intellectual into such direct conversation with the personal is something I seldom do—on paper, anyway. Of course, these facets of my life are in constant dialogue, feeding and fueling one another in complicated but necessary ways. To be an Indigenous scholar, to be Yellowknives Dene, to be grandson to Marguerite and Napoleon, comes with the deepest felt responsibility—an ethic of obligation, reciprocity and also *fight*, that I aspire to fulfill every day. To lean in and put my ear to the sounds of my territory forces me to bear witness to the violence of noise and to all the disruption and dispossession it represents. It forces me to expose all of my senses—the rawest of nerves—to the many layers of loss and grief that my community have confronted since the discovery of gold decades ago. But what it has also done, and most importantly so, is open up my own understanding of Dene sovereignty and the dynamism of its realization and expression. It has revealed to me in the most visceral ways the failure of efforts to silence us on our own territory. And while we indeed bear the affective weight of colonization, and the unjust burden of tending to the wounds of colonial ecological violence on our land, we are still here to provide that care.

GLEN SEAN COULTHARD

"Listen closely and you can hear another form of harm caused by the increase in mining development on our territory: the acoustic violence that accompanied the mine's operation."

"The interregnum of revolt follows an evolution of despair so long and excessive, the corrective asks for everything."

CANISIA LUBRIN

A Catalogue of Bridges

CANISIA LUBRIN

Prelude

This is an attempt to sound the break in our big world of unnatural things. The republics of dysfunction that we call life today, as Frantz Fanon warned, are less the point than the price of the ticket of reform. Now we have a word for it: neocolonialism. In this world, we know that one of the first casualties of putting bandaids on the fetters of tyranny is the mincing of nearly all language into euphemisms. Because story, or more precisely, narrative, is the great catalyst. Since the Age of Discovery™, colonization's wardrobe of euphemisms has spun mission after mission: civilization/christianization™, humanitarian™, manifest destiny™, right of return™. If one must attend to the deepening crises of this early twenty-first century in more than merely an oblique fashion—with what voice could a map of these discontinuities speak of collapses in the social, ecologic, political and cultural orders of the world? This is an incarnation of a poet's nightmare, impossible and (un)bearable to accomplish, both archaeologic and futuristic. Museum and workshop. So it's important to sound the break, to call things by their true-true names.

This practice of being, noticing and refusing is necessary in a world shaped by conquest and the abundance of its divide-and-conquer classrooms. This rippling expanse that further guarantees the incoherence of history. In this, survival is more than seductive. It is a way of seeing symptomatic of a victory, typical of the in-between—the spaces for making and unmaking in the present tense, the activities that must strike the end blow to modernity. Where armies of its defenders come with legends about unconquerability, the dispossessed always seem to find persistence in the present continuous tense that we call *rising*. Could it be enough, then, simply to expand an oblique determination to learn from the linkages, the ongoing dialogue between periods of revolt, such as we have now? Another age of revolution. Another more menacing foe.

In the broader global struggle to assert human dignity into a coexistence of genuine stewardship, I would like to leap at every wound even without the salve, even with my arms not big enough. But sound is large enough, so let us sound. Even when this feels like a necessary failure: these acts of naming in the interregna of the ailing world. Here and there, in the narratives of others and of ourselves. This act is standing face-to-face together in a ghostly room, to be firm in the overwhelming inertia of the present fascisms. This act, more circuitous than I would prefer, is a story of assemblage. In this way, I think always of a before.

Before—which implies consequence, not apart from etymology, such as that of the word *capital. Capitalis*, the medieval Latin from which *capitalism* is derived, means "of the head." And when joined with the word *pars* refers to the principal sum of a loan. Over time, "capital" evolved to refer to stock, merchandise or funds, and in the nineteenth century the modern term "capitalism" came to describe the system of private ownership of the means of production. By then, this system's dependence on hierarchy, property and exponential labor evolved the terms by which wealth was measured (a head of cattle, or a city, or a loan) into a global system of colonial expansion, state and private enterprise predicated on race. The evidence of a world inaugurated by chattel slavery engulfs. The uncountable-inarticulable indices herald.

Before the value-making categories of light and dark. Then and now. Win and lose. Stories and history. What was before escape, or a naming of just cause? Before species? Before the need to be buffered in the heady comfort of *fate* best suited to the less skeptical of the species. What was before the necessity of ideas? Of deep consideration, questions, fantasies, answers, hypotheses, debates. Before horizon, land and sea, open and close, time and speed. The Haves and Have-Nots. Our living and our dying. Before the intelligence of the species. Before anthropology and erasure, god and philosophy, subjugation and dominion. The moving picture, the calendar, the clock, the wheel. String for bass and banjo. Fire, food and sleep. The snare, car, train and the plane. Before cities, ballots, bombs, war and profit. (Dis)ease, cures, drum and book. Genocide and memorials. Need, invention and legal codes. Before the foolhardy work of searching the enemy's eyes for a mirror. Before the note, chorus and bridge. Before mapping oneself, forgetful and flawed, in every direction of the future. Before us and them. Person, thing. Safety, threat. What is more complex, more durable? Bonds that precede and what follows. Here, in the bold log I admire (the grand auditorium inciting the present concerns), *before* can mean the galactic likelihoods of atoms and the ideal conditions following star and planet and millions of years compounding into eyes, ears, thumbs, lips, minds, feathers, hides and scales. Past and future in the interval that C.L.R. James evinces in *The Black Jacobins*, that "when history is written as it ought to be written, it is the moderation and long patience of the masses at which men will wonder, not their ferocity." Visions of waking the life that wants for good. And then considering the breaks, the ego's blunt instruments, its appetites for destruction, the greed and morbidity of a meager imagination seeing only itself. Though barely knowing itself. Before regard for seedling or fiber, dust or water. What can be misused, bought, sold, discarded without a thought to what keeps on. What must be remembered as the true cost, (before and after) the unveiling, extending, damaging work that ends and begins other worlds? The tools and methods for attending to memory and transcendence, which is another name for the unknowable, or what must happen next. The body. The body. The instrument so sensitive to the horrors that it compels the present address.

12 PRENSIP BOIS KAYIMAN
(12 PRINCIPLES OF BOIS KAYIMAN)

1. Tout moun sé moun. Pa gen moun pasé moun.
   All people are human. No person is better than another (or is more human than another).

2. Tout moun gen plas yo anba syèl ble a.
   Everyone has their place under the blue sky.

3. Si gen pou youn gen pou de. *If there is enough for one, there is enough for two.*

4. Chak moun gen fason pa li pou li lapriyè. Respekte fason chak moun lapriyè. *Everyone has their own way to pray. Respect how everyone prays.*

5. Sa nou pa konnen pi gran pase nou. *What we do not know is greater than us.*

6. Nan pwen anyen nan lavi a ki pa gen règleman. Se règleman ki bay lavi a ekilib. *There is nothing in life without a law. Law gives life balance.*

7. Pa defèt ekilib lavi a san rezon. Moun, ki mal deplase eleman yo, ap rale malè sou tout moun. *Do not displace life's balance without reason. People who displace their essence bring misfortune to everyone.*

8. Tank n ap aprann, se tank n ap konnen kòman pou nou respekte ekilib lavi a. *The more we learn, the more we will understand how to respect life's balance.*

9. Pa janm manje manje bliye. *Never forget things easily.*

10. Toujou sonje: fè koupe fè; dèyè mòn gen mòn; pa fè san inosan koule; pa lage chay nan men

manfouben. *Always remember: No matter how tough you are, there is always someone tougher; there are more mountains behind mountains; do not shed the blood of innocents; do not have careless people bear responsibility.*

11. Veye! Lènmi Bois Kayiman ap vin sou tout kalite non, ak tout kalite rechany pou yo tire revany. *Watch out! The Bois Kayiman's enemies will come under all types of names, in all types of clothing for revenge.*

12. Malè yon eritye ki bliye esklav fè Bois Kayiman pou moun k ap sèvi Bondye pa lote moun nan mitan bèt. *Shame on the heir who forgets that slaves made Bois Kayiman so that people who are serving God may never again be put in packs among animals.*

1. Tout moun sé moun. Pa gen moun pasé moun. • *All people are human. No person is more human than another.*

The predictable cracks in the membrane that is the upkeep of the status quo arrives, as we expect, with its sterile pretenses. They seem without an official timetable, but we know their rhythms. Dammed by the long durée of stately crisis after stately crisis, a great enormity has broken again. Here I resist reproducing the usual index: the calendar of human history where ruin buries ruin. No list will exhaust the sophistry of the broken and popular.

Here is a gradient, nonetheless, to set the scene:

Daily life in sixteenth-century San-Domingue, now Haiti. You have managed twenty years on Earth before learning the life-altering sonographs of captivity. The covert trailing of an approach in the bush or on the road. Or the battle cry scoring the wind before blade and the shackle, whose sounds differ depending on their design. Iron shackle for the rub and clatter (like dub) of metal weight on the locomotion of limb. Or crab rattle shackle, for the metal balls sounding the captive's every move. Other shackles, of bells or spiked collars, to alarm two ways: to dissuade captives from becoming escapees, and, prior to life on the plantation, to locate those who annulled the slaver's version of their lives and would be called the *runaway*. At the slave castle, more bells will blotch your ears, joining you to the calamitous losses of others newly captive like you. At the end of the world you'd known all your life is a new, vaulted relation in the hold.

There is no place where these troubles have been fixed. Good-enough attempts to administer lasting solutions are still far off in a future also beset by the spectacles that will be made of those crucial moments—triumph and failure—bridging cyclic histories of conquest to their phonetics of too much.

To be here is simultaneous sociality. The sound of gunfire and metals scoring flesh mark your passage to unbelonging. A world beginning with rulers and producers of The West™, and in that world you are the proven and dangerous limit to the ideology of bondage. In the hold, they invent the idea of themselves as "Man" (the ultimate and only), chosen by divine credit to be carriers of civilization and Christendom. This fallacy is boomerang, and for another four hundred years no tactic of assimilation and inclusion will patent a scheming counterpoison. More than flesh in the hold, you carry a *before* that will transform into battle cry, the wood-against-wood creaking of a ship's groaning womb. The stinging bass of the ocean against the ship's hull is presage. Before Glissant, you emerge from "the abyss" into a short fugue of sleeplessness that cannot stand for life on the black soil where you will be herded for the sugar mill. Day over day, come the sails of harvest, there will be no single event to which you can be compartmentalized. You will cast a line down the centuries, arm to arm, one back to the next, mending the fabric of a kinship from Motherland to a "New World" grave from which, one day, someone who will speak with a voice like yours will answer to the name: Dutty Boukman. Will answer to the name: Cécile Fatiman. Will answer to the name: Nanny of the Maroons. The coming marronage on which your very *life* will depend is the wellspring where Aimé Césaire will recall you late in the twentieth century, as though by a conjuring before history, with the words:

> I hear coming up from the hold the enchained curses, the gasps of the dying, the noise of someone thrown into the sea . . . the baying of a woman in labor . . . the scrape of fingernails seeking throats . . . the flouts of the whip . . . the seething of vermin amid the weariness. . . . So be it. So be it.

For you, only twenty, life expectancy is twenty-three years. Before the enslaver brands you Caliban, your time on a ship at sea, stripped of all life-giving tenses, had taught you the Noise of rebellion is bond. Against and inside the architecture of catastrophe. For three years, you come to know la Karäibe, the Caribbean, the West Indies, if not merely, then mostly, as the severing of land from its ecosystems of relation, its routing into setting for imperial barbarism's most encyclopedic displays. During the three years you survive, 150,000 more just like you arrive on San-Domingue, but there is a world into which you were born free, and in which you had become knowing. Inside that expansive catalogue, the grammars of black living you remember is this *life,* that its world precedes.

By now it is the 1700s. In San-Domingue, second only to Brazil, the population of the enslaved outnumber slavers ten to one. The archipelago that is your station has suffered the genocides of its Indigenous Peoples so that a sugarcane economy, now at its peak on San-Domingue, can boast the envy of imperial powers worldwide. What is not in your hand? What don't you know? What can you trust? What language will compel liberation, and what sounds its dimensions? Already, you know the strange has its place. Further down the watercourse, for instance, Rinaldo Walcott, born in Barbados, will say "emancipation is long," and another descendant born in St. Lucia will agree, that in the infernal log, who can split the tragedy of Emmett Till's killing from the alleged whistle raced in what Cornelius Eady, born in New York, calls the "brutal imagination" of white America forty-two years before this sentence?

The intervening years will mark interruptions, turns and (re)tunings of the everyday registers of the plantation. What was once the snare-driven plow and the cutlass for the harvest and processing of sugarcane is hushed in the sugary drawl of the cube-on-cube syncopation of calypso, emerging hundreds of miles away on another plantation in Trinidad and Tobago. In two centuries, along the same continuum, the Mighty Sparrow will sing of a society of post-independence women forced into prostitution, *ten-to-one is murder*, and Christina Sharpe will detail the longtail of those "monstrous intimacies" in her 2010 book. The calypso chantwell's creole is criticism. Calypso answering the art of the body in limbo. Opening to repair's signature sounds: refusing the carceral in all its forms. Too, calling that wayward cousin, soca, into the fray. The important bodily memory of the Middle Passage, the waves that scored your survival, your severing from home: head to spine, hip to feet. Its refractory, brackish idiom caching pleasure, ecstasy and sensuality in the very sinews of the diaspora. Whose ears are primed for the bean-on-bean semitones of coffee into the slow-reverb and roll of konpa? And not too long ahead, the subterranean dirges of breeze through indigo, San-Domingue to Louisiana and beyond, that will saturate the blues. In that interval, Daphne A. Brooks is writing *Liner Notes for the Revolution* where this sentence appears: "For the women below, in every sense of the word, sensory revelations are the key to social revolutions." Another ordinary day and you hear a friend bawl: "Beware the dogs of war, disease, and the phonemes of cruelty in their euphemisms." You both convulse for the branding: hot operation (burned at the stake), raising them up (crucifixion), mowing the lawn (incremental collective punishment). The mercenaries, changing names though not stripes, have mastered their craft. What lexicon for this vile music? What appropriate response?

—

Where you and I can go together might be antidote because, at the interregnum, going together proves the only recourse. By now, we know the stories well. The desired lift doesn't always follow the mutiny. Civilization's chronicle is a revolving door of human concerns told and retold in every medium and foreclosed where narratives of superiority and self-congratulation echo and comingle inside a suspicious paradox of ethics and value. That tyranny happens somewhere away, especially where you claim lineage, family, beloveds, should not verify it here. It is to be the death knell for its ending anywhere.

Repetition forwards more than a time signature in these accounts. Celebratory notes in the wake of such history belong to survivors of the ruptures, to those who risk a shareable life, as Rinaldo Walcott signals when he asks, "What might it mean to live a life, if we can't risk desiring and working towards utopia?" The extralegal infrastructures of nihilistic violence will produce failures, setbacks and even vengeance, which all negate inaction in a world of massive inequity and chance.

Where the histories of the oppressed are plagued with common and strange atrocities, dates readily eclipse other dates and what endures, passing from mouth to mouth, hand to hand, ear to ear, house to house, stream to sea to cloud, is the largesse of our interior life. More durable than the diminishments of enforced explanation, the scarring of sanctioned disclosure, called surveillance, that interior life does not need indexing. It is bodily felt and lived, resounding at this interregnum.

Today, all the world's emperors gather in their most prized nakedness, with contempt for the masses, and they rend, openly, the social fabric on a global stage. That ruling class continues to deny the reality they orchestrate, one ordinarily understood, even and especially by children, as profane. So unafraid of the retribution of the overpoliced, underpaid and overworked, they mock the masses deprived of healthy communes and affordable housing. They gut educational institutions, starve conservation and environmental programs of resources and repeal their regulations. They privatize public goods and defund social services. Will the understanding that none of this is sustainable come to overwhelm in the people that which enables the illusion of the arrow of time? That which demeans and guarantees their bootstrap aspirations? Will the zealous corruption and greed veiling the body itself in spiritual deformities fall away if one refuses to be satisfied with waiting for the system to fix itself, with believing that it will? Who will learn the burden of the dispossessed which, equally, unveils the body? What can threaten the ruling order's traditions of exploitation if not direct hit after direct hit to their gains? This interregnum is thick with calls to boycott, divest and sanction. Some have worked; others lag for the inaction of many and of governing bodies. Symptomatic of the ruling order's delusions of grandeur are the ways they foreclose their own imagination, and in this way, their playbooks never change. This might be little consolation to everyone but the strategist guided by an ethics of coexistence.

2. Tout moun gen plas yo anba syèl ble a. • *Everyone has their place under the blue sky.*

As it is with oral histories given scant attention, the catalyst of the Haitian Revolution is cast as folklore and carries the heft of an astral place.

Marlene Daut details how:

> Dumesle's *Voyage dans le nord d'Hayti* . . . is the first known written source to document the contents of Dutty Boukman's speech and contains the transcription of it still referenced by the vast majority of scholars who discuss the ceremony today. That "Dumesle's retelling" focused on how the lyricism of poetry is restored to this world historical event. . . . The Haitian poet-historian Dalmas recalled that it was "toward the middle of the month of August 1791 when cultivators, manufacturers, and artisans from several ateliers in northern Saint-Domingue reunited in the middle of the night. In the midst of a violent storm, they met up in the thick forest that covers the sommet of Morne-Rouge and formed the plan for a vast insurrection, which they sanctioned with a religious ceremony." Here is the magnificent story as it was rendered by Dumesle into a poem:
>
> Through the furrows by the lightning traced,
> Where the glow of a hundred lights eclipsed burn,
> Groups of the oppressed assemble in silence
> They bow their heads invoking assistance
> From the God, who, in a brilliant people awakened,
> The illustrious Spartacus, that valiant slave

The interregnum is drenched. The slaver's reign of terror must be drowned. Counterweight to their historical present, another descendant would draw this ceremony into 12 Principles. No disguising the has-been. The propaganda that gains the signature of The News™ by denying the achievement of Bois Kayiman might annotate institutional authority, but its 12 Principles are fountain. What Michel-Rolph Trouillot in *Silencing the Past* calls the "unthinkable revolution." A poetics of repair the way water is, the way poetry is. The sonic plays a major ritualistic role charging voodoo priestess Cécile Fatiman, and a poetics of repair rides that leap of incantation "through the furrows by the lightning." If poetry means to open more fully into our precarious transit between life and death, it lifts the resolve of the multitude. As water is, poetry, likewise, does not end at utterance. Here I imagine the gathering at Bois Kayiman. Among those present, poets, transmitters of ordinary and scarce language (the language of good dreaming) to the many. The poet who grows from the earth waits in the world's garnet of feeling to trawl, at the needed time, the spirit for what is warm and pulsing, for what compels, hemorrhaging the blueprint of the burdensome. The plantation must give up the ghost of history to the chaos of its rebels' interior lives. I imagine in that mythic clearing at Bois Kayiman, those gathered call each other poet, and in that tongue, they steel away to the ritual of keeping alive in themselves that ecstasy of freedom-dreams. Freeing mentally, and across the expanse of another century, where Harriet Tubman will find railroad and star, and Miss Lou will sing in the clearing of another stage: "Sun-a-shine but tings noh bright /[...]/ Rain-a-fall but dutty tuff!"

The consequence of living beings trusting together the life-force of the voice is the opposite of social collapse. Let me call them the poets of ceremony at Bois Kayiman. Imagine them, following Saidiya Hartman's critical fabulation, how they intimate far down this now-familiar trans-African diasporic watercourse—"the Atlantic . . . / the beginning of music," as in Dionne Brand's *Nomenclature.*

Here, let me speak the radical poetics of possibility in the Haitian Revolution and its voodoo ceremony at Bois Kayiman. Voices winding a music of repair is this threshold of a collective vision emerging to bring an end to the dread of chattel slavery in San-Domingue. In the shared language of poetry alone, the poet, perhaps, is merely one who seeks, listens and transmits the many names of our experience, in the languages of feeling. The heart that knows the point at which what is clear *does* sing. So does the heart go ahead of the need. So does the heart recalibrate what the drive of human ambition so adeptly reduces to mere function or *utility*. Use that abandons life and living for short-term acquisition. Reminders of the poetics of the woods, the world beyond the human, the corner, the street and cloud. The clearing, as in Toni Morrison's *Beloved*. Liberation need not be declared because it is already evident there at the center of the otherwise.

There is no need for ballads detailing the humanity of Bois Kayiman's protagonists. It is where "everyone has their place under the blue sky." Not the cliché of untroubled times, but the realization of a sociality in the brightness of the liberty still to come. I am drawn now to imagine the qualities of their voices altogether, their bodies enraptured because they were together. The visions their creole invocations instruct because they went together. The welling of their lifeforce because, together, everything—in that instant—seemed possible, practical, and right there. Together: earthly, down home in the now fused and performative exchange of voice and storm. This singing is discovery as much as time travel. A record of a before-time since most of the enslaved at Bois Kayiman, as with most slave colonies, had had a life in Africa in their own languages and worldviews and cultures. They did not need to imagine the condition of freedom. The source of their courage and will to reject captivity is no real mystery. Faced with such danger, anyone, anywhere will fight. Obedience to dictums of "what is meant to be, will be" is encouragement to those slavers who had judged the enslaved in San-Domingue not capable of the very humane activity of refusing their deracination. Russians, take note. They, likewise, could not anticipate the clearing at Bois Kayiman. Everywhere now are stories of the rising successes of the dispossessed rejecting the habitual colonial ideology that demands, even today, accepting oneself as the prisoner of history. Making oneself the prison of history. This refusal is a sounding of an ethics far away from the supremacist theologies that underscore racial terror, even now.

One who must fight their dispossession has to be more medium, more ordinary savant than archivist because the conditions that lead to revolution are always too severe for reasoned, logical appeal. The primary fluency of the language of freedom begins with a reclamation of bodily autonomy, even ephemerally, even with the legacy of violence disfiguring the flesh. A restitution of nonviolence in that milieu is the crude preference of those who benefit from the cleaner violence of civility so crucial to the ranking order's longevity. In the fugitive music of poetry that enraptures the gathering is the ineluctable fire of the language of the streets. This collective striving is in the expressiveness and legibility of the ambient and singing crowd, and when the singing stops, the people carry and share its quality of duration and defiance. What is in the strategic genius of the maroons is also in the peasant who knows the song is the suturing signal that the future of a truly liberated world is also one in which there are no more masters.

3. Si gen pou youn gen pou de. • *If there is enough for one, there is enough for two.*

Now I must tell you about Natasha. With a silent tongue and a quiet ear, she entered the world as though to break a kind of sense the hearing world had been primed to expect. In her mother's own words, Natasha's tongue was pinned to the base of her mouth. And by a similar calculation, she could offer less to the science of sound. It was sudden, when loud music sprung a singer into her day. She stood, leapt, a small crowd gathered on our hillside road parting for her. She danced and danced—an hour gone easily by. I might have missed the great lesson of this if not for the discography filling my childhood from soles to head. Among others, Whitney Houston and Nina Simone, Mighty Shadow, Fela Kuti, Sessene Descartes. Sounding into the mountains that would link me and Natasha, my deaf relation, to sea and valley. How roomy, our shared love of music? The answer is a chasm between express and possess. The answer is Natasha, like a seasoned dancer, her body following nearby speakers, their frequencies sprouting through air. Vibrations of song after song waking her, skin to depth. In this way, with her unique sign language learned during her brief years of formal schooling, a hybrid of basic American Sign Language mixed with gestures invented collaboratively with her family (their vocabulary as eccentric and physical as Natasha's choreographies), Natasha explained, dance was proof of life. So she did not care that others were scandalized by her dancing. I had learned from them some of this sign language, which I have now, to my penury, forgotten. But this is how she explained to me that if the music is played at a high enough volume, she feels it in her body, and it is like being possessed. It was as though, as Saidiya Hartman writes in *Wayward Lives, Beautiful Experiments: Intimate Histories of Social Upheaval*, "if she could feel deeply, she could be free. She knew that beauty was not a luxury, but like food and water, a requirement for living." The beauty of the interregnum where her (in)ability to hear and speak broke the sense-making habits of the crowd—tuning us to wonder. Natasha's dancing required total abandon. It was wild and fibrous with affect. Apart from the ordinary vernaculars of the 1990s Caribbean, Natasha's moves (and perhaps, her life) were lessons. The human body unhindered by restrictive judgments can defy sense. Uncowed by a sanctioned respectability, it can be sensitive to the frequencies of sound waves beyond the sensible physical function of organs. The idea of the single being, the European man, is mere industry. Perhaps the most profitable in the history of the world.

In chapter two of *The Black Jacobins*, titled "The Owners," C.L.R. James writes that "long before 1789, the French Bourgeoisie was the most powerful economic force in France, and the slave trade and the colonies were the basis of its wealth and power. So, the slave trade and slavery were the basis of the

French Revolution." With that revolution underway, enslaved people in the Caribbean would reach neither for the luxury of nonviolence nor the symbolic, nearly silent intrusion of a petition. The enslaved in San-Domingue recognized their own fire in the intensity fueling the actions of the peasants in France. Only a turning toward life at world's end could launch the revolt that would come to influence many others and strike fear in the mean hearts of enslavers all over the colonial world. In the French colonies, especially in Haiti, Guadeloupe, Martinique, St. Lucia, at the time—colonies solidifying the dominion of the French—the straitjacket of colonial (dis)order had been breached. The brutal machinery involved in the naming of the world from the centers of corrupt power need always be continually examined as the groundwork of resistance. From the top down, inequality breeds contempt but also inspires the revolutionary passion of the dispossessed who recognize in the idea of The Universal™ the fortification of, for instance, the economic fatherboards requiring the enslavement of children in the cobalt mines of Congo, the exploitation and displacement of millions from Sudan. Surely, we're unsurprised by scenes of the women of Sudan, of the people of Congo reaching out to the world from the hollow of capitalist abandonment that flung them into the streets, the dynamism of their African harmonies, their refusals ricocheting like Langston Hughes's negroes singing of rivers. The lament of wounded kinship (re)sounds across the centuries. This practice of negation is heirloom and repetition.

Here, to think of abundance is to admit that it might be nameless. Be *before* naming, but freedom is the choral density of continuing. That Africa, one of the most resourced continents on Earth, can be ravaged by colonial exploitation is not coincidence. So the women keeping score of the violence that hates their life, that poisons and impedes their children, also command a resourcefulness to match questions of our full future lives. In the face of the femicide that is crucial to the playbook of war are the larger troubles that head militarization. In the commonness of the upheavals on the African continent, a world structurally organized by extractive and separatist dogmas meets globally embodied organizing for prohibition: for women's rights from South Africa to Argentina to America to Iran. More: the Arab Spring, Summer and Winter uprisings; plants uprisings from Georgia to Ukraine to Myanmar; 2018–2022 Latin American protests from Haiti to Chile, Paraguay to Venezuela to Panama and Peru; revolts from Palestine to Greece, Sri Lanka to Sierra Leone, Hong Kong to Iran, Ukraine to Mongolia; student protests from Canada to Nepal. What famine in Bengal, in Ireland, in Sudan and Palestine have to do with the Black Lives Matter movement around the world in 2020. In these freedom songs which have no other register but the gathering that looks like poetic justice, what is still to be relays what is sensitive to the demands of the lapse. A breaking from form in the shrinking individualism that typifies the world of capital, and which destroys true sociality.

Here is Aimé Césaire in "Cahier d'un retour au pays natal":

> Je déclare mes crimes et qu'il n'y a rien à dire pour
> ma défense.
> Tr.: *I declare my crimes and that there is nothing*
> *to say in my defense.*

Another from the translation by John Berger and Anna Bostock:

> My mouth shall be the mouth of misfortunes which have no mouth, my voice the freedom of those which break down in the prison cell of despair.

Such insistence embodies the creative expressions of the gathering at Bois Kayiman. Indigenous and ancestral knowledge schemes used to transform something that should have destroyed them into another legacy. The world, though weaponized and abused, is not estranged from its inhabitants. Its suffering is ours, though it will outlast us. We've watched, the past two years, Palestinians refusing colonial empire's vision of annihilation inflicted on them. Digging out of rubble after rubble, kin after kin. With their bare hands, over and over, salvaging those whose condition could be their own in the same instant as they try to reclaim them from crater after crater left by a bomb. The persistent harmony and DIY rhyme of reaffirming linkages across time and space, across "bridge[s] over troubled waters." Similarly, the voodoo ceremony at Bois Kayiman, consigned to myth in some official circles, may well have transmitted beyond their own quarters the sounds of life that the first participants of the revolt recognized as ushering the world they believed was possible, that of a liberated San-Domingue. The phases toward winning such liberties are not linear, though where language leads, structures follow. The conduits are made for the transfer of energy, and the touching and touching transformation requires. Slow to catch and quick-moving when it does in the absence of a hero or main character.

The rhythm of life rooted in good feeling. In a glimpse of the total outline of the wild world. Of water, dirt and air in the chaos of a shared Earth. What is a claim of coexistence if not our shapes inside the motion we call time? Its practices convey, in each of our own primary registers, the livingness that challenges the disorders already waiting for us beyond the summons of birth. Something before the word was with anything. None of this relies on the philanthropy of the moneyed of the species. This is the abundance that reaches through to rhyme and repair. Call and response in the long history of a planetary epic. Our entrance into being the antiphonal call and answer of the cosmic in us. An exercise in the potency of a relational lifeforce. Foreshadowing what we count on that will be the genius of the social mind and heart. The sinews, the currents, primed for our passing through such a life as this. Weathered over and over in the ruptures of intelligent life, the body is vocal with irony and openness. Life so intelligent it might see itself the least at the center. But among other beings who do not need or declare the "Rights of Man" to be open to the non-obstruction of the activities of life in the margins. The paradox is as much the spendthrift of our semantic morphologies, as the deepening preverbal feelings that sound and stretch even silence into meaning. Our sensorium since our beginning does not bend to judgment or discrimination but demands knowing ourselves in the relational forces of the storying species we are. What else keeps everyone available and defiant in their own registers holding still this knowledge? To rely on something that insists on its mystery is to commune with abundance. And everybody knows to appreciate the score.

4. Chak moun gen fason pa li pou li lapriyè. Respekte fason chak moun lapriyè. • *Everyone has their own way to pray. Respect how everyone prays.*

> "The god who created the sun, which gives us light, who rouses the waves and rules the storm, though hidden in the clouds he watches us. He sees all that the white man does. The god of the white man inspires him with crime, but our god calls upon us to do good works. Our god who is good to us, orders us to revenge our wrongs. He will direct our arms and aid us. Throw away the symbol of the gods of the whites who has so often caused us to weep and listen to the voice of liberty, which speaks in the hearts of us all."

This was the prayer, or Boukman's spell, spoken at Bois Kayiman. This mode of passion belongs to the self, mystified in the way that C.L.R. James hails as being true of "a phenomenon noticed in all revolutions," where the oppressed seek to destroy their oppressor because they face an unrelenting force. What is prayer in this but the daring performativity in the idea of the power of one's sovereignty? It may have little to do with belief and much to do with imagination. Little to do with opinion and much to do with imagination. Already it is possible to understand prayer as synecdoche for visioning what is yet seen as impossible. More to do with mood than with activism. The history of conquest is the story of someone arriving in a "strange land" with an insatiable lust, with a claim of totalizing power, by divine authority, to civilize, to free, to educate, to defend. It is understood by now that this is cover for pillaging, thieving, and turning everything good in life into a proprietary exercise, by leveling untold horrors at those who would impede.

In the face of this, a summoning.

October 9, 2025, the eve of a Nobel Peace Prize announcement, the depraved clowns at the cantilever of empire declare again that a ceasefire has been brokered between the leaders of Gaza and Israel. I swipe down to a video of two Gazan children standing next to the sea and speaking into a camera held by the girl, who tells the boy, "We got a ceasefire," to which the boy returns, "Oh, we hear this all the time. I don't believe it." I swipe again to video by Palestinian journalist Bisan Owda, whose "Hello, everyone. This is Bisan from Gaza, and I am still alive" remains one of the echograms of the Palestinian Genocide's latest chapter. Here she was again: "Hello, everyone, I am saying this sentence not as an update but as a result: *I am still alive.*" One journalist's survival opening her reports of collective struggle, in which we, the people, countries away, recognize a common historical force. For two years amid computerized mass killings and communications blackouts, Bisan's sentence arrived with the steadiness of the tide, like air breaching a horizon every few days.

5. Sa nou pa konnen pi gran pase nou. • *What we do not know is greater than us.*

Is Bisan, like Natasha, one we must observe in the eagerness of what we do not know? Of what the roots of goodness demand. What I had learned through the invitation of Natasha's deliberate meanings fortified with her dancing. Another world of feeling in the frequency of music in the air. Natasha, like Bisan, could communicate everything with her body, even with the great silence of her singularly vibrant mouth. Bisan's repertoire on October 9 includes this polemic: "We must not be naive. No one must engineer our happiness, engineer our feelings and our relief that finally, children are not being massacred while they sleep; . . . everyone working on the peace plan has been manipulating you and will manipulate you." Along with the boy talking with the girl in the first video, Bisan would be proven right mere hours later, an apartment in Gaza City bombed with more than forty people inside, shattering a new hope. Soon more videos with voices cutting across each other clipped with prayers will cast a dim mood across the virtual and physical realms.

If it was inside the wind-rattled living room of my childhood that a ten-inch color TV served as a beginning, then I must suffer the reductive activity of naming it so. 1991. News of unrest elsewhere had filled a day and my sisters' voices with chatter about riots, arson, looting. In the evening, a broadcast—Michael Jackson singing a line no more human than "it don't matter if you're black or white." Though only a child, I recognized, in Jackson's intensity, the discontent stretching his voice, demanding all my attention. In that voice was something less strange than unnameable. So I focused my novice thoughts on something more manageable: the music video's strange opening sequence. The singer, the poetry in his voice, his wrists turned up and out at a world he knew very well to guard against. In my little ways of seeing, I wondered what was in the elsewhere my sisters were on about, and whether those eight words in Michael Jackson's chorus were the fighting words they had talked about all day. I sat transfixed for the whole of that eleven-minute video, agreeing with everything, even the autopilot of that maroon loveseat, how it flung the white man into an African safari where lions with gaping mouths lay waiting, apparently, unbothered by the white father in his loveseat, who'd moments earlier decried his son for wasting time playing Jackson's track in the middle of white suburbia. White America—flung that far out through cloud and comet, wind and condensation, by this same son's defiant strum of a guitar.

It would take many more years for me to understand why *this* song, and why *this* man was singing it. That a lineage of defiance lay in its staccato. That this had trained me to receive, four years later, that lyric of indictment in Jackson's 1995 album *HIStory: Past, Present, and Future, Book I*: "I know if Martin Luther King was living, he wouldn't stand for this." The video for "They Don't Really Care About Us," imbued in the vernaculars of sonic defiance, was appropriately filmed in Brazil, the last place on Earth to abolish chattel slavery during that age of revolution.

These childhood scenes, as though conjured, came to mind again as I watched Ryan Coogler's deeply researched 2025 film, *Sinners*, an homage to black sonic and intellectual history and life. At the midway mark of the film is the juke joint scene that works like a calendar through the evolution of black (mostly) American music and its foundational registers. In the scene, blues is groundwork for overlaying soul, jazz, Irish folk music, gospel, rock and roll, Chinese folk music (Xiqu), West African griot stylings, and hip hop (including trap and G-funk), with sensitive attention to the transcendent properties of the genealogy. This sociality of sound disavows the monopolizing force of institutions on the corpora of human activity that comprise culture and assemblage. Rooted in the senses, the power of sound constitutes transcendence as embodied memory. It transmits a knowledge that isn't predicated on the fallacy of supremacy or the singular orthodoxy of the book. The scene begins with humming (*hm, hm, hmm, hMM, hm, hM-hm*), transgressing time and space, harkening back to the plantation and the founding of the blues. The audience itself is conduit, available to sonic dimensions of the incomplete desires of generations and therefore requiring the participation of the whole social animal across time and space. In the scene, many liberatory forms of dance crisscross into a visual lineage peopled by generations brutalized by racism, symbolized in the figure of the vampire. The interregnum of revolt follows an evolution of despair so long and excessive, the corrective asks for everything.

The clarity of the principles of Bois Kayiman condenses into the realm of contemporary struggle, a vigilance against the weaponization of memory. It is a real-time prism for the assemblage of masses at sites of interruption around the world. Language is being co-opted in real time, and the very foundation of meaning is contested. The stories that emerge, the songs and chants filling the streets of islands, towns, major cities and more places matter in the face of the impunity that has turned the world into a giant shopping mall, the human no more than a till. Homo Capitalis is Insatiable Man™, who claims, voraciously, the knowledge of all things for itself. In this flattening of the world, it is possible to put all intelligence in the service of ruin.

Equally, the inventive orchestrations of a chorus pushing past such spectacle expresses the incomplete activity of a quest for moral clarity toward intervening into the debased catalogue of Homo Capitalis with fairness, liberation and the possibility of a good life. The gathering is the result of going beyond argument and rationale. Togetherness without a safe harbor is homed in the flesh, and it is through the flesh that we are animated despite the illusion of conclusion in the official record. What autonomy of the heart answers the interregnum, the rupture opening to action, creating the conditions of transformation? In the dread crucible of the modern, those I call ancestors undertook this history, the mind rewilded from the mystery of folkloric encounter. The folkloric being our collaboration in the known and unknowable.

6. Nan pwen anyen nan lavi a ki pa gen règleman. Se règleman ki bay lavi a ekilib. • *There is nothing in life without a law. Law gives life balance.*

After almost two years, the ferocious spectacle of mass killing in Gaza would finally include famine. But before that: the language of blast after blast, bombs bearing the names of enthusiastic proponents of war. The hungry humming of drones and their quick-tempered sniping. The near silence (through my phone) of babies left to rot in NICU units. The flapping of evacuation orders dropped from planes. In and out of tents in refugee camps, screaming and praying and cursing. New weapons tested, shredding limbs, shredding whatever is left. Mothers, fathers, any relations, picking up the pieces of their beloveds to carry in cloth, plastic bags, buckets, even on pieces of shrapnel large enough. This insistence on finding a burial ground of nowhere safe. None of this is metaphor.

But for all my keeping watch, my listening for the death rattle of this world, for the inducting sound of a better world, I am at this interregnum of disaster orchestrated by humans, yet again, with what I had discounted as a useless activity, but which had now become my road to this writing. And what is this writing worth? Do I anticipate a scholarly public is waiting or in need? Still, I failed to understand immediately why famine seemed a terminus for many. The emaciated bodies of children, of Gazans, finally convinced many more in the unwilling spectatorship to break their public mask of silence. Famine during genocide becomes a last station for the body already asked to bear too much. She who is famished must accept the evil of the world that has abandoned her and, at once, is staged in the enigma of the relief of death. Such a body becomes too wasted from within to recognize and respond to nutrients and their uses. A ghostly state that cannot be understood as belonging in a benevolent cosmos. This is the opposite of what the girl I had known, dancing in all her deafness, had caused me to feel. More than an absence of delight, a complete denial of life, similar in lesson, nonetheless. Unlike with Natasha's dancing, my characterization of famine as the body's teaching feels profane. And it might be. But it is my thinking through. How the famished body becomes too human to carry a sonic register, something accrued with age and measured, it seems, in the essence of aliveness, the vitality of nourishment. The corollary is to death, that which has leapt ahead of its bounds. Might it mean everything is too intense, intense enough to render the body that experiences famine utterly still, and in a strange duality of encounter, compels the witness still available to the heart's ethical chords to act. One cannot stay hidden for long in the silence of a fear damaged by malice. So, should the ability to make famine into abstraction be available if the only result is relief in the psyche of the observer? Whatever the work, I had a hard arrival. If much of our sense of humanity and morality materializes in the body's physical languages, then our psyches cannot bear to gaze at the gauntness and the near-mythic syntax with which starvation speaks. It is too explicit. The silence of it so loud and wounded. There it is—the vile balance of an unspeakable natural law.

7. Pa defèt ekilib lavi a san rezon. Moun, ki mal deplase eleman yo, ap rale malè sou tout moun.
• *Do not displace life's balance without reason. People who displace their essence bring misfortune to everyone.*

In a world also marked by extinctions, the balance of life's spontaneity with enough research, context and intention buffers against dejection. About history, what the liberation for a people heavy on the antiseptic calories of simple, easy, sameness looks like? The contemporary need to flatten everything in accessible soundbites? The logic of a market holding a gun to every trader's head? About beauty, necessity and the coolness of odd and bizarre things, what is antidote? What has gone wrong in the world if freedom must be made a project over and over? Dionne Brand reminds us of the tragic poetics of the slave castle door in *A Map to the Door of No Return*, which she writes 209 years after Bois Kayiman: "I cannot go back to where I came from. It no longer exists. It should not exist."

These notes follow the cultural and psychosocial chain reaction of history's exploratory events, though, uniquely, every locality will have its own verses, its own notes. What has gone right for the project of freedom to be taken up globally? For the deployment of concrete and abstract techniques, from the surreal to the defiantly real in confirmation of and contradiction to modernity's toll? And it terrifies the tormentor who cannot accept such evidence of unbroken spirit, unbroken will into militarizing police and weaponry powered by so-called AI. The roll call sounding the interregnum lodged in the cyclic nature of time is much too long for the hour. So, a few more for all with a street to sing on: the youth of Madagascar; music teacher Ahmad Muin and his students singing at the pitch of the drones under a tent in Gaza; activists on the Sumud Flotilla singing antifascist songs. The pivotal turning point in the years-long Sudanese revolt against a corrupt government and social deprivation, the twenty-two-year-old engineering student Alaa Salah standing on a car in the middle of the road, singing of women's liberation, a sea of protesters around her with drums and a spreading fervor. Such scenes repeat.

8. Tank n ap aprann, se tank n ap konnen kòman pou nou respekte ekilib lavi a. • *The more we learn, the more we will understand how to respect life's balance.*

Yet again, *the fix* is not a static outcome but a reasonable paradigm, a set of conditions within which to strive for restorative relation. A fact within which, here, now, an imaginary of radical care enacted by masses of people in present tenses around the world could be the closest we've come to confronting the structural tyrannies of modernity in many decades. No surprise that the backlash has, this time, criminalized those who insist on telling a bolder and truer story of this world by gathering in the streets. That all the heroes of the racial order are lionized and the frameworks matured to critique them are being banned. Here is the minor detail in the cosmic wild of learning how to change and change and change: to reconfigure around life from within. To distinguish ourselves from the narrative of containment that makes the simulacrum. For we cannot be caught in effigy. In the vapid transparency of commerce that conscripts all of life into transaction. Nor can we afford to be transfixed in the logic of despair that empire and its ambassadors declare the total perimeter around our lives. This interregnum is a *yes* to *no,* to a chorus of *NO*s against endless servitude and being deposed in a world of inequity. Cuba to New Guinea to the Northwest Territories.

The mother of Malcolm X was born at the turn of the twentieth century in Grenada. White plantation owners still held most of the country's economic power, and access to education was only just opening to children of working people. Only to those unaware of the history of revolutionary women in the region would it be a surprise that Malcolm X grew up to be a revolutionary himself. That Assata Shakur had anything to do with the revolutionary spirit in the music of Tupac Shakur.

Years before, Marvin Gaye's record label initially rejected *What's Going On* for its politics. Gaye, who would grieve the label's decision, "I'm not a poet, not a painter, but I can do it with music," demanded the release of his now classic album. Necessary cultural expression for Gaye; mere dogmatic fodder for the capitalist enterprise funding its release. Not long after Nina Simone's "Mississippi Goddam" and Billie Holliday's "Strange Fruit." A quick time between Bob Dylan's "Blowin' in the Wind" (of the Jim Crow South) and Sam Cooke's response in "A Change Is Gonna Come." Countermeasures from inside the imperialist abattoirs run by the shady dealers of popular culture thriving on the ignorance of the masses, and on racist doctrines that deny the arts their place in the pantheon of activist discourse.

The resounding of this world, its vital practices of naming and sorting little-known and lesser-felt things about who we are or might be, such a catalogue is in the 12 Principles of Bois Kayiman. The ideas in them "risk utopia," a principled turning away from a deadly solipsism toward a shared, sounder world. Each of these principles insists on personhood beyond time and map. Each anticipates, not just the otherwise, but another freedom, one without dispossessions.

9. Pa janm manje manje bliye. • *Never forget things easily.*

There is no simple category for this fractal record. What it demands is that we think differently about our relationship to the world. A genuine corrective for the climate crisis, unparalleled inequality, overlapping epidemics of what Ruth Wilson Gilmore calls the "helix of organized abandonment and organized violence." Imagine what is yet unsurpassed: stolen and hoarded wealth used to correct shared historical and cultural tragedies. If we were too passive about our own lives, this would be lodged forever in the hypothetical and would be left for irony to judge. Too, we recognize the interregnum as a space to gather provisions, to resign what needs resignation. The interregnum for ending and unveiling. The afterimage for a tenacious, sobering clarity, everywhere obvious in the interregnum of protests, revolts, refusals, happening now.

10. Toujou sonje: fè koupe fè; dèyè mòn gen mòn; pa fè san inosan koule; pa lage chay nan men manfouben. • *Always remember: No matter how tough you are, there is always someone tougher; there are more mountains behind mountains; do not shed the blood of innocents; do not have careless people bear responsibility.*

Resistance needs no throat. It lives in blood, swelter, hurricane and fire. What good grace that it is unrestrained by the extremes of its opposite. It is the throat.

It will work with whatever vessel is available, whatever modes it finds, and it asks that you break the demand to see yourself first or at the center of panoramic violence. With whatever is capable of sounding a tomorrow, it will work. To draw a larger radius of participation into the fold of all being and living things, it will work. To unsound the dead-end myths that demand beauty in the rubble, it will work. The enemy of liberty hates that it is disfigured more and more by the indomitable spirit of those it tried to destroy, though it has its own negations—it won't give up its cruelties. Never willingly and never without a cost of unspeakable suffering. Such that it uses its institutions to criminalize the refusals of those it oppresses. Wet'suwet'en, Antifa, Baka, Algonquin, Black Lives Matter, Palestine Action, Amazonian Land Defenders, among many others. And what it does not achieve with systems of apartheid, it depletes with judgments of transaction. It coerces by attempting to smooth over with language, rebranding, for instance, bribes as "economic reconciliation." Those it does not demolish, it builds more and more prisons to hold. It tries to sink into sea, drown with blood, pulverize in deserts, poison in air.

The anarchy of sounding the hard business of living and surviving the worst day of your life again and again. Sound—for the long charting work that must follow the uprising. Sounding as defense against the amnesia of turning away from the hard things. Remember that in November of 2023 a group of Gazan children stood together in a press conference to address the world in English, the language of the colonial entity at the root of their displacement: "We invite you," they said, "to protect us from the bombs falling over our heads." Over the next month, steadfast in its tradition dating back to 1972, the US would veto another of several UN Security Council ceasefire resolutions, thirteen to one, plus one abstention, amid the deaths of another four thousand children, with thousands more maimed and wounded, including those given a newly invented marker, WCNSF (wounded child, no surviving family). From the safety and comfort of my living room in the core of the empire arming the fighters, I wept, wondering if any of the children of the press conference were among the dead and wounded. They who understood already that repair is a collective responsibility against the governing plots of a civilization in which a livestreamed genocide does not halt business as usual. Nothing we'd tried at our distances had stopped the bombardment. Not the protests, not the boycotts, not the symbolic and the concrete maneuvers. When the Sumud Flotillas would sail to the shores of Gaza with humanitarian aid during the Gazan famine, the activists aboard, they, too, would be detained and abused. The story at the interregnum is less a conclusion than a shifting of the gears.

11. Veye! Lènmi Bois Kayiman ap vin sou tout kalite non, ak tout kalite rechany pou yo tire revany. • *Watch out! The Bois Kayiman's enemies will come under all types of names, in all types of clothing for revenge.*

Chestnut Revolution, Orange Revolution, Arab Spring, Slipper Revolution, Cedar Revolution, Saffron Revolution, Umbrella Revolution, Green Revolution, Purple Revolution, Yellow Revolution, Singing Revolution. Mountains behind mountains.

Tracing the Haitian Revolution to a history of life-affirming ideas rooted in African cosmogony would be easy if one means to evince a lineage of the propagators of societal change made evident at Bois Kayiman. Ubuntu and other such unifying principles of liberation ultimately argue against the demand that a brutalized people always be virtuous in their struggles. In "Silence for Gaza" translated by Sinan Antoon, Mahmoud Darwish laments, "Time in Gaza is not relaxation, but storming the burning noon. Because in Gaza values are different, different, different. /[...]/ The only value for the occupied is the extent of his resistance to occupation. That is the only competition there. Gaza has been addicted to knowing this cruel, noble value."

12. Malè yon eritye ki bliye esklav fè Bois Kayiman pou moun k ap sèvi Bondye pa lote moun nan mitan bèt. • *Shame on the heir who forgets that slaves made Bois Kayiman so that people who are serving God may never again be put in packs among animals.*

Before Toussaint Louverture would utter the words "the roots of liberty spring everywhere." Before Jean-Jacques Dessalines said "leave nothing white behind you." Before Jean-François Papillon would argue for the plantation economy to continue in Haiti under a new democratic order, a ritual involving the sacrifice of a wild boar, the endurance practices of marronage and its ingenious strategies, and a song led by Cécile Fatiman were the aggregates opening a moment of rapture. An expression of what Fanon means when he writes, "I should constantly remind myself that the real leap consists in introducing invention into existence" (p. 29). It is not singing as an instrument of proof but confirmation itself, speculative dreaming, opening out and out and through. Marvelous and unprecedented, wild, mysterious. From where we gather, the ceremony at Bois Kayiman is what Nathalie Joachim calls "story as the definitional autonomy of personhood" for the dispossessed, portal of what Daphne A. Brooks would call "the conjuring in the archive." Though what had followed the long tail of enslavement and revolt in the preceding century were laws forbidding music (especially drumming), singing, and the enslaved gathering, especially for ceremony, Haitian peasants alchemized courage and won their freedom beginning with singing. The violence it took to overcome the extremism of chattel enslavement was sure. The fire it drew was sure. The punishment of its daring still ongoing.

It's not hard to imagine the ruling order's puppeteers sipping their brandies, laughing without moving their mouths. Laughing at the plight of the underclasses. Declaring the corridors of resistance that open incrementally always too small, the people too overburdened in austerity economies, too sedated on the gospel of affirmation to transform the status quo. The people can survive only so long before the conditions that demand their "moderation and long patience" force them into negation. This axis of domination further depends on the middle class, apportioned gospels of aspiration, rations of civility, tax-paying pride to be always exactly the cudgel that keeps the undercommons in their place. Here, the middle class's every intermission from the naive spoils of their vote trusts a manipulation called reform that is little more than dispensations of the same dysfunctions under new names. In this interregnum there's no global minimum wage. Eight men own more wealth than half the world, and 327 million workers are paid at or below the applicable minimum. Here, comfort means what is maintained by state apparatus, the militarization of quotidian spaces—and security is the violent hegemony of the police, whose only language is force. Their every grammar, every vernacular loud with the anguish of the dispossessed. But flip the page. Constant rebellions and the victory of the Haitian Revolution dealt the unexpected blow to the age of conquest that cemented modernity's abject operating system. The enslaved ushered a new period, mutilating prevailing modes of business as usual, which determined that The Slave™ (by narration, never by ontology) would be pressurized evermore into property. So it goes for how the world is made and unmade.

Perhaps everything elemental is against erasure. Another polity of breath, voice, the audacity of self-determination come to the fullness of the gathering. The new and old places for risk and collaboration. Against casting the future in the funny amber of revisionism, where for protesting genocide and war, your government will designate you a terrorist. Fissures run up and down the social order now, and trust in institutions of authority, whether the news, the church and even the university, is everywhere broken. The importance of a collective social vision relies on more than belief; it is strained and collapses when public servants, nurses and teachers have no choice but to strike over and over, when power grids fail because of carelessness, when airplanes drop from the sky because of profiteering, when airport authorities lose contact with planes because of government negligence, when parents are jailed for lack of papers proving their residency, when masked secret police abduct people just going about their day and place children under ten in handcuffs, separate them from their parents, and are then forced to defend themselves in court. Appeals to the institutions that uphold these systems will only reinforce the sources of these mere symptoms of structural breakage. Repetition's potent transmissions across the scale of time turn history, itself, into cyclical host-prison. And the more extreme the systemic collapse, the more extreme the response of the masses must be, the greater the personal and collective risk, and the greater the potential for transformation.

Today, as drones serve a dual purpose—their buzzing for psychological torment and their bullets for death—the vision in Bois Kayiman's principles insists on relation, which cannot be assured the moment what is expressed corresponds in magnitude to the rehabilitation of the psyche from the hold of Homo Capitalis. The opposite of social collapse is living beings expecting together the lifeforce of collective expression. A poetics of refusal, notations for beginning again.

CANISIA LUBRIN

"The interregnum of revolt follows an
evolution of despair so long and excessive,
the corrective asks for everything."

"The executioners take language for
themselves and have mastered its use.
The poets know that language is a living
thing and a collective possession."

MADELEINE THIEN

"No Sword nor Any Book"—On the Quiet of the Library

MADELEINE THIEN

This morning, in the city library, a child hurried past me as if pursued. *Where to begin*, her eyes, filled with longing, seemed to say. *Where to begin when I am already out of time?* Around her, people appeared and disappeared between the rows of books. They turned the pages of newspapers or sat daydreaming in the afternoon light moving through the rooms.

I come to the library once each week. I like that books arrive and depart as if through a train station, that a book will be propped up on a kitchen counter or splayed open on a bed or forgotten in a bag for three weeks before returning to its usual place on the shelf. I like that anyone can arrive with a borrower's card and no money, that people can drink their fill from the water fountain, or drowse, however briefly, in a quiet corner. I pick up recent arrivals whose pages, already worn thin, will soon be retired, and old books so crisply new I wonder if any reader has ever turned their pages.

Up on the fourth floor, I find the book I'm looking for, John Berger's *Here Is Where We Meet.* In the opening pages, Berger speaks to his mother, who, although she has been dead for fifteen years, appears in the city of Lisbon. She has been sitting on a bench watching him. His mother tells him, "Everything in life, John, is a question of drawing a line, and you have to decide for yourself where to draw it. You can't draw it for others. You can try, of course, but it doesn't work. People obeying rules laid down by somebody else is not the same thing as respecting life. And if you want to respect life, you have to draw a line."[1]

Her words, which I do not fully comprehend, touch a nerve. For a long time I have been thinking about conscience and its relationship to grief, speechlessness and fear. Fear has long been a part of me, twisting through my lungs. Lately, this disturbance, the knowledge that I bear responsibility for acts which go against my conscience, has grown. The word *conscience* stems from the Latin root *conscientia*, "a joint knowledge of something, a knowing of a thing together with another person."[2] I am surprised to find that the root conveys the opposite of loneliness: knowledge within oneself and, also, knowledge with others.

I circle the streets of the library, wondering.

In November 2002, I was twenty-seven years old and living with three friends in a shared house near the University of British Columbia. I had just finished graduate school. One afternoon, my mother left me a message on the answering machine. I believe it was a Wednesday. That evening, she joined me and my roommates for dinner at our favorite Korean restaurant. She arrived, as always, smiling. Even though we had nothing special to celebrate, our mood was celebratory. The next morning, my mother left for a work trip to the interior of British Columbia. The day after that, my sister left a message on the answering machine, her voice breaking, begging me to call her. I dialed her number but no one answered. I remember that I climbed into bed and, unsure what to do, opened the book that was nearest to me, Cees Nooteboom's novel *All Souls' Day*. I had only thirty or so pages left to read. Seven pages before the end, the phone rang and I got up to answer it. My sister told me that police had come to her door to inform her that our mother had died in the night. She had not felt well the previous day and had gone to the hospital. In the afternoon, she returned to her hotel, having been diagnosed with pneumonia. Her colleagues said she seemed in good spirits but tired. In the morning, when she didn't appear, they asked hotel staff to unlock the door. Inside, she looked so peaceful they thought she was sleeping and began to apologize for disturbing her. But she was gone. She had slipped away sometime in the night. At the age of fifty-eight, she had gone to sleep and never awoken.

Many things happened in the hours and days that followed. I remember that, when I was able to hold her hand again and tell her that I loved her, I knew she wasn't there. This was a new quiet—to be in the room with her and yet to be alone. Until then I hadn't known that when we are in the presence of another human being, we can hear the hum of their soul, a soundless sound, and when that presence is gone, the silence is palpable and undeniable.

At the end of 2002, I moved out of that shared house. I packed the Cees Nooteboom novel I had been reading, despite being certain that I would never return to those last seven pages. Before departing, I noticed the steady red light of the answering machine. My mother must have left other messages and her voice would still be there. Impulsively, I removed the microcassette and put it in my backpack. My parents had never owned a Super 8 or a camcorder, and we did not have any videos or recordings; and our family photo albums, too, were lost to me. But I never grieved those things. I had writing. I had the refuge of my imagination. In the years that followed, in the stories and novels I wrote, my mother appeared in different guises, in a way of standing or turning, a certain blouse, a small detail. I sought her living presence in these continuous transformations.

The years passed and technologies changed. Voicemail arrived and then mobile phones and smartphones and texting. I never owned another answering machine. I kept the microcassette in a small box alongside some of my mother's CDs, a notebook from elementary school and a favorite dress my aunt had sewn for me when I was small. For the next twenty-three years I moved continuously. I put this box in various closets and, often, in the basements of friends. At some point in my thirties, I emptied the storage space I had been renting. I gave away hundreds of books but I held onto this small box.

In 2024, the parents of my beloved passed away after long and complex illnesses. My father had died, holding my hand, six years earlier. Our parents, children during the Second World War, survivors of famine and bombing campaigns, survivors of civil war, men and women who had left behind homes, countries, friends and dreams, departed this life. Afterwards, the two of us began to let go of things. We said to one another: We don't have children, so who would want our belongings? Better to make decisions now so we don't burden our friends, the poor souls who will be stuck with the loose ends of our dying. And this back pain we're starting to grouch about, this arthritis and bad vision, it's only going to get worse. Shouldn't we lighten our lives and our spirits? We made our wills and joked that it was the most romantic thing we had ever done.

One day, while clearing odds and ends out of a borrowed basement, my beloved called me. There's a box here, he said. I think it's your childhood things.

Oh, I said. Put it aside. I'll deal with it later.

He brought the box home. When I opened it, I felt the past covering my feet and then my knees, and rising ever higher. The little dress my aunt had sewn. A school notebook. The microcassette from that long-ago answering machine. It had been twenty-three years since my mother's voice had reached my ears.

Oh well, I said. There's no way to play it. Who makes answering machines anymore?

We could find one on eBay, he suggested.

The tape is probably unreadable.

Maybe, he replied.

The next day, while I was trying to do my taxes, he came in and placed a microcassette player, a Dictaphone, on the desk.

Where did you find that? I asked.

I guess I had it all this time.

Does it work?

It works, he said.

I'll try it later, I said, and went back to doing my taxes.

I returned to the library and wandered its streets. I saw people looking skywards and inwards and into the pages of time. I saw people rushing to collect a book that might help them bake a cake, plant cucumbers, speak Spanish or discover a swimmable lake not too far away.

I found myself thinking about something my beloved had said to me that morning. How quiet the bookshelf is, he had said. How many voices and words it holds and yet how mute it is.

At home, our shelves are full of things I have not read. But here and there are books that have accompanied me for decades. There is a richness to their quiet. Alive with ideas and images, bearing anguish or transformation or wonder, they are patient and also fragile. If I put my ear to the shelf, I imagine that I might hear the tide of all of us, forever arriving and departing. We didn't have books in our home when I was a child. Books were luxuries, but I longed, in the middle of the night, to reach for them, to walk along their passageways and hear their voices. I hated having to return my library books. The stories I loved didn't provide answers. Instead they offered me companionship, the chance to be with another human being and even, perhaps, to become another self. No matter the secrets, sadness, violence, poverty or the ache of childhood, a book held out the promise of another way of living. Eventually I learned that, when I had to return a book to the library, this was no loss. They had taken root in me and I could find my way back to meet them again. Their quiet was my quiet, their muteness was mine, and this friendship could never be taken away.

When I was in high school, we moved to a condominium outside the city. During these years, my mother and I lived together as a unit of two. Money was a constant worry; my mother's health was declining and her job stressful. Most mornings we would get into her car, merge onto the highway and, in bumper-to-bumper traffic, head downtown, where she would drop me off so that I could catch the bus to school. My mother loved to sing, and during our commute we listened to her favorites, Whitney Houston, Bette Midler, Connie Francis and Teresa Teng. I cannot say she had a beautiful voice, but it was warm and loving. In the car we could speak freely to one another. When my mother spoke of me to others, she called me Maddie and, rarely, Madeleine, but when she spoke to me directly she called me Med and, sometimes, A-med. During winter and summer breaks, I tagged along on her work trips to the interior of British Columbia, or into the forests of Vancouver Island, or to visit her many scattered friends in many scattered neighborhoods. When we argued, it was about politics. I believed myself to be a radical. She knew everything about me but I barely knew her; she died before I relinquished youthful self-absorption and the constant need to run away. I have long dreamed of being in the car together one last time. I do not want to dwell on her workplace environment, or the long years when she was mercilessly bullied by her managers, or when she had to take stress leave, or when shopkeepers refused to serve her or spoke to her with contempt, or when colleagues or acquaintances mocked her accent. She worked hard, staying in her office late into the evening, eventually making friends with the night cleaners, who were, like her, immigrant women. I don't want to remember how she told me, almost lightly, as if she wanted me to both hear and not hear what she was saying, that she was at high risk of a heart attack and that I should be prepared. Later on, when she read my first book, she told me that it had made her feel less alone. What more could a daughter wish for? Spoken more than twenty-five years ago, these words still keep me going. I suspect I have heard her crying more than anyone else. I remember that sound. But most of all, it's her laugh that still resonates across the years. But no, that is not entirely true. I see her smile. I see the curve of her body, I see the whoop of joy, but I cannot hear the laughter I remember.

At home, I study the Dictaphone on the desk. How strange that a sound so long awaited might arrive too soon. I chide myself for being so unready. I tell myself, It's a piece of magnetic tape that may or may not still contain her voice. It will certainly break the moment you hit play. *Be careful.* I had been twenty-seven when I took the microcassette out of the answering machine and I am now fifty-one. I realize that in all the years since, I have always made sure to keep one message from my beloved on my voicemail. I never delete it unless another one has arrived. A habit formed, like all habits, by subterranean layers of longing and remembrance.

On my weekly trip to the library, I borrow several books, but the one I open on my return is one that has been on my bookshelf for a decade, *Touch*, by the Palestinian writer Adania Shibli. I have multiple copies of this book because it has transformed me in ways I find difficult to explain. The cover is blue. It is seventy-two pages long. I open the novel and read its first line, *The big brown water tank stood on four legs, appearing from a distance to be an ant standing perfectly still.*[3] I keep reading. I keep reading until all the pages have passed through my hands.

The girl at the center of *Touch* is never named and never speaks in the first person *I*. She sees, hears and touches, and little by little, year upon year, her sensory world expands.

Among the first things she perceives are colors. Sky and land are blue then orange then purple, colors which dissolve and transform and which together form a wholeness. When the sun departs, darkness covers everything. This deep black, she thinks, this color of night, existed before the sun and will exist long after everything else disappears. "So God," she thinks, "was behind the darkness, unfolding it and folding it again whichever way He willed."[4]

At times, the girl is desperate to escape "sounds that wanted all the ears."[5] She takes refuge in the family's car in order to shut out the noises, which, because she is ill, cause her physical pain. Loneliness "always saved a place" for her.[6] She wonders at the "big sounds" smothering the "little sounds" and longs for "the paradise of silence."[7] Her palm, placed against the chest of a neighbor, hears "the noise of his heart, which again disappeared when she moved her hand away."[8]

The novel opens like a hand. Its five parts—colors, silence, movement, language and the wall—extend and shape her existence, and contain questions she cannot voice. Instead she reaches out instinctively to touch what is outside her: the movement of the sun and its shadows, the smoke from her father's cigarette, the sky that evades her touch because it is "too soft," this softness which is also the property of the sun and of the face of another human being.[9] She touches the lingering cold that "caused bodies to move involuntarily," or the mirror that stands in the middle of a room "revealing the beauty of whatever went on in front of it."[10] Not everything is within reach. Her mother's smile is so rare that it surprises and puzzles her. And touch, too, sometimes transmits unhappiness and injury.

When her brother dies suddenly, his body is brought home in a car and carried inside on a cot. Color, silence, movement, language and the wall remain the texture of the little girl's world. Shibli writes:

> The girl followed the cot as it was carried from the beginning until it reached the mother in the sitting room, where she sat all alone. The brother fell from the cot into her lap. After some time, his face got wet because the mother's eyes were directly above it. Rather than wipe the wetness from her face, she wiped it from his. She moved her hands from the eyes to the cheeks, to over his mouth: over and over, slowly.[11]

The girl cannot stop her eyes or ears or any of her senses from bearing the touch of this world. Moment by moment, these sensory encounters bring forth her existence. The novel is spare, so spare one can almost feel the breeze as it moves between the lines. The instabilities of sight, sound and movement are joined to the instabilities of believing, knowing and judging. "The sky," the girl observes, "had not changed its silence or its shape or its position after the brother's soul rose up to it."[12] Where, then, is the soul that has departed? As she grows older, the girl discovers five rows of books in a glass cabinet in the house. When she pulls open the cabinet, "its sound was like that of a stone at the entrance to a cave."[13] The turning of a page scratches the air. Words "stacked neatly on the lines" bring sensory experience beyond her immediate surroundings, and she names this experience abundance.[14]

Touch is what we each receive, and what life grants us. Lights, images, tastes, sounds—they are all forms of touch.

An image, writes Gaston Bachelard, resounds within us because it has "touched the depths before it has stirred the surface."[15] I think that our depths and surfaces sometimes meet, but other times, they unfold in different realms. Sometimes we imagine we plumb the depths of our souls, we take the measure of our heart, we search inwardly and submerge into the unknown. But perhaps we have it upside down. Perhaps it is the depths that are making an attempt to reach us and we—our selves, our noise, our fear—who stand in the way of their passage.

The novel's five chapters, each no more than a dozen or so pages, gather forms of touch. Everything that surrounds her—a blue plastic bag, a demolished building, a tea tray, the sound of a whistle, the rays of the sun, her own shadow—is the shell of something else. Shell upon shell, she comes into contact with the boundaries that circumscribe her existence. Which kinds of touch lead to knowing, and which to love, and which to harm? Which must be protected by secrecy or even silence? We move our bodies through this world, and our hands can give so much and also destroy so much. Eventually the girl marries and leaves her family. On her departure, she carries her loneliness with her, "embracing the wall with her eyes." This wall "encompasses all vision," and when she looks at her sisters, "the girl's embrace of the wall intensifies. . . . Between the bumps on it she strings lines in every direction. . . . Between the bumps she strings lines with her eyes. She cannot escape it."[16]

Like the colors she first perceives—the colors of sky and land which dissolve, transform and together form a wholeness, mortal things in an immortal world—the girl leaves without leaving. There is no going back. Yet there is only return. The lines of existence are made of such things.

In a late work, the poet Mahmoud Darwish writes, "Like a small jar of water, absence breaks in me."[17]

The microcassette and the Dictaphone sit on my desk as I go about my days. The books beside them pile up, and when I open them they sound the tide and tidings. None of these books are new to me. I am in a period of rereading, an interregnum between what I once understood and what I cannot yet see. I hope that those who once taught me, who long ago came like strangers and gave me bread to eat, will find me again. There are pieces of music a person listens to repeatedly, sounding their depths, and there are images that never cease to return. Twelve years ago, while visiting Vancouver, the city of my childhood, I looked out the window of the SkyTrain and saw a mother and child waiting on the opposite platform. The back of the girl's head reached her mother's stomach, and her mother's arms rested lightly, tenderly, on the girl's shoulders. The girl was looking out, her expression pensive. I could see tears rolling down the mother's face. What had happened? Were they escaping pain or was it inescapable? I began to weep. The mother did not let go of the child, even to wipe away the tears which continued to fall. The train doors closed and I was pulled away. I turned my head to keep them in my sight. But already they were gone.

The mother and daughter have never left me. The girl must be in her twenties by now. And the mother? I see them everywhere, in places both near and distant; they linger in my vision. I feel that I know that mother and I know that daughter, I know the glass that separates us, the movement that brings us into one another's view and then slides us away.

Today the silent book on my desk is by Bertolt Brecht. Years ago, while writing a novel about the Chinese revolutions of the twentieth century, I read and reread his poems. He torments me, he comforts me, and he insists that if I am to be what I say I am, a writer, I must find the words. It is not enough to say that I am grieving or that I am speechless. In his poem "To Those Who Follow in Our Wake," he writes:

> . . . He who laughs
> Has not yet received
> The terrible news.
>
> What times are these, in which
> A conversation about trees is almost a crime
> For in doing so we maintain our silence about
>   so much wrongdoing!
>
> . . . .
>
> They tell me: eat and drink. Be glad to be among the haves!
> But how can I eat and drink
> When I take what I eat from the starving
> And those who thirst do not have my glass of water?
> And yet I eat and drink.

I would happily be wise.
The old books teach us what wisdom is:
To retreat from the strife of the world
To live out the brief time that is your lot
Without fear
To make your way without violence
To repay evil with good—
The wise do not seek to satisfy their desires,
But to forget them.
But I cannot heed this:
Truly I live in dark times!

. . . .

You who will come to the surface
From the flood that's overwhelmed us and drowned us all
Must think, when you speak of our weakness in times
    of darkness
That you've not had to face:

Days when we were used to changing countries
More often than shoes,
Through the war of the classes despairing
That there was only injustice and no outrage.[18]

The book sits open on my desk, a quiet gaze. In the silence, I tell Brecht that I have a story to tell him.

Once there was a man who experienced debilitating pain along his trigeminal nerve. A breeze touching the side of his face would cause pain so unbearable that he would be "crouched in profound suffering, almost immobile, afraid of triggering pain."

The man could no longer bear his suffering. As a last resort, neurosurgeons lesioned cells in his frontal lobe. Two days after the operation, the man appeared smiling and relaxed. His physicians asked about the pain. "Oh," the man answered cheerfully, "the pains are the same, but I feel fine now, thank you." At first, his doctors were bewildered. But soon they realized that, in lesioning these cells in the brain, they had separated pain from suffering—they had separated the body in pain from the self who experienced it. The damage to his trigeminal nerve was still generating pain, but his brain was no longer evoking, or able to evoke, his own suffering.[19]

During the years when I was writing about the Cambodian genocide, I learned about another kind of distinction—how bombs and torture and man-made starvation inflict a different kind of suffering from tornadoes, earthquakes and events we deem acts of god. The suffering inflicted by one human being on another tears the soul apart, for the victim faces the unseeing eyes, or the all too horrific lucid eyes, of the perpetrator. Human beings suffer psychological torment when they know that another human being, or group of human beings, has singled them out for harm. For so many, the last touch is a cruel one, the touch of one who inflicts pain, who severs life, the killer who believes themself to be a god.

The cellular material of our synapses and neurons is the substrate of both our agony and our indifference. Are such in-built structures changeable, I wonder. For instance, can someone who is unmoved by the murder of one thousand children be moved by the murder of twenty thousand children? Or a hundred thousand dead human beings? At what number do the dead become human again? Or is this a pointless question?

Conscience, that wordless torment in the gut, a clarity of the heart, a joint knowledge of something, a knowing of a thing together with another person: Where does it come from, what is its reality? How do we come to utter the words we speak?

I ask Brecht, who despite his principles and his love, fell silent when those around him were purged and murdered, to tell me about the life of the conscience. But another book resounds in my thoughts, and another voice, John Berger speaking to his dead mother. "Everything in life, John," she repeats, "is a question of drawing a line, and you have to decide for yourself where to draw it. You can't draw it for others. You can try, of course, but it doesn't work. People obeying rules laid down by somebody else is not the same thing as respecting life. And if you want to respect life, you have to draw a line."

I read and reread the page, struggling to understand. "The number of lives that enter our own," writes Berger, "is incalculable."[20] Perhaps, I think, his mother doesn't mean a line that is a partition, a wall or a divide. Perhaps she means a line from one to another, a thread joining one life and the next. Perhaps this line is a distance crossed or a drawing near or a form of touch. "Here," Berger repeats, "is where we meet."

The Dictaphone and microcassette sitting mutely on my desk are oddly reassuring. I tell myself: Do nothing. In fact, I joke to myself, borrowing the words of artist Song Dong, make this a *do nothing garden.*[21] This tape might contain the only recording of my mother's voice in the universe, and if I try to play it and the tape breaks, that's it—end of story. Better to keep her voice in the realm of the possible. I pick up the microcassette, which is absurdly small. I remember the clack of the eject button and my younger hand reaching into the answering machine. My hands are beginning to wrinkle now, they look like my mother's hands. One day, if I am fortunate, these will be the hands of a very old woman. In fact, with every passing year, my face and my expressions resemble my mother's more and more. Or perhaps they always did. Maybe I only recognize the likeness now, when the face that haunts my dreams appears in my reflection and the mirror seems to hold two silent figures at once.

A sense of calm enters me as I contemplate the muteness of the bookshelf, holding pages written by the dead and the dying. They ask questions I have not thought to ask. The bookshelf searches me; it floats through my sensory and intellectual life and my dreams.

In November 2002, I was reading a book while I waited for my sister's call. During that hour, afraid to step forward in time, I hid myself inside another person's imagination, inside Cees Nooteboom's *All Souls' Day*. When the phone rang, I marked my page and went to answer it. Moments later, knowing my mother was gone, I moved the book from my bed to the desk. Later I moved it from the desk to a shelf, and then into a suitcase, because I was moving to the Netherlands, the country, as it happened, where Cees Nooteboom lived and worked. For decades, uprooted between countries and apartments, I carried this novel with me but did not open it. And then, fourteen years after my mother's passing, I took it down from the shelf, climbed into bed, found the page I had marked and began to read. The ending of the novel is about departure. The protagonist, recovering from illness, observes a painting hanging in the room where he sleeps. This painting shows a graveyard "so big that you couldn't see where it ended," and in this graveyard are women who "didn't seem to be walking, but, rather, to be floating or drifting between the tombs, beyond the cypresses and the acacias—a dream world stretching out to the horizon." Hundreds of women gather in this cemetery, chatting, embracing and laying flowers. The painting is said to depict All Souls' Day, falling each year on November 2. "Perhaps," Nooteboom writes, in the last pages of the novel, "the graveyard itself was floating, sailing like a ship of joy through the air. Any moment now it would rise up and take the women, the children, and the flowers" on its journey away from here.[22]

I finished the book and set it on the bed. At length, I unmarked the page and returned the novel to its place on the shelf.

Nooteboom's image of the women, the flowers, the children and the ship has stayed with me. It has echoed in the world my mother left behind in 2002, in the images proliferating over the past twenty-three years, of graveyards so big you can't see where they end. This image has hovered beneath my own stories and novels.

I think it takes a certain kind of muteness to be a novelist, a muteness that is a form of speechlessness and therefore speech by other means. The hope that if we accept this hollow, this wordlessness we carry, another chorus—the women, the children, the flowers—will fill our ears and take possession of the page. But now I remember something else: After my mother died, I stopped reading fiction. Novels felt too contained and also too indirect. Too contrived and yet too evasive. The ability to breathe inside them, which had come so effortlessly when

I was a child, stopped, like a door abruptly slammed shut. And then after two or three years, this feeling of claustrophobia subsided and fiction again found its way into my hands. What changed and then changed again? Not literature itself. It must have been my own ears and what they were able to hear. Perhaps they, too, were learning to contract and expand like lungs.

I returned to the bookshelf this morning and sat in silence, resting my head against its questions and its doubts. Should I put the microcassette here, I wondered, next to the poems of Yam Gong and the novels of Yoko Ogawa? Wouldn't my mother feel at home beside them? Isn't the bookshelf, too, a resting place, or perhaps a state of limbo, for voices departed but not yet dissolved, lives which continue to press against our own?

I imagine that when I remove a book from the shelf, the ocean will come rushing through the gap. Here it is, I think, the world, the space between two books, the interregnum, the quiet that threads between the sounds.

Years ago, the poet Mahmoud Darwish wrote that the world had yet to hear the voices of the Trojans. "Homer is the glorious song of the Greeks," he wrote. "There is no doubt that the Trojans would have expressed things differently, but their voice was forever lost." Darwish's words make me think about the way we listen. I imagine that over the course of a lifetime, the ear must grow weary, and the mind, too. We grow used to the sounds of the world, and our listening attenuates. But some people, and some writers, until the very end, never cease to be sounded out by the world. I think this is a very rare thing.

A few years before his passing at the age of sixty-seven, Darwish spoke to translator Mohammad Shaheen about the many friends of his who had died what he described as "ordinary death." I could not, he says, "erase their names and telephone numbers from my notebook or from my memory." Darwish spoke of a recent heart operation which he had barely survived. He continued:

> I wrote my long poem *Jidariyyah* about this experience. Every death is a first death, and for this reason it surprises us and we are afraid and saddened. We have to put out of our minds the fact that death is our constant companion and the fate of every being. We have to put it out of our minds so as to know how to live, how to work, and how to search for a significance of our lives. But we must also remember it from time to time so as to ease its swiftness a little, and to be humble.[23]

In *Jidariyyah*, or *Mural*, published just before he turned sixty, Darwish describes anemones. These flowers, he says, are opened by the wind. But what wind brought him to this life, and what wind is now carrying him away? If I must go, he thinks, then let me go "to the highest mural."[24] The mural, something affixed to a wall, or a painting created directly upon a wall, is the surface upon which the poem is laid. Wherever the wall stretches, the mural will find expression, yet what is painted there belongs to more than its containment.

Mural, described by Darwish as an epic hymn, is a book-length poem that spans a thousand lines. Translated into English by Munir Akash and Carolyn Forché, the poem begins like this:

This is your name, she said
and vanished into the spiral corridor . . .

I see a heaven within reach. A white pigeon's wing
    lifts me toward
another childhood. I didn't dream that I had been
dreaming—everything is real.
Clearly, I laid myself to rest and flew.[25]

The figure of Death draws near, offering Darwish a liberation that is also an ending, but its work is interrupted as the poet wakes once, twice, three times, back in the hospital room where a woman counsels him to be worthy of what he will soon dream. Perhaps he has become only "the dreamer's speech," he thinks, carrying nothing but his name.[26] "You are my reality," he says to his name, "I am your question."[27] Name and self are united and disjoined: "What's the use of my name without you?"[28] "O my name," he grieves, "where are we now?"[29] Learn this name by heart, he tells himself, "and don't dispute with it."[30] He continues:

. . . besieged by dualities, I am a life-long traveler
    to my interior.
But life deserves its obscurity and its sparrow.
I was not born to know that I will die, but to love
    the innermost of God's shadows.
Beauty leads me to the beautiful,
and I love your love unchained by its essence
    and attributes.
I am my own double.[31]

Years ago, in a story called "The Colour of Trees," Lebanese novelist Rawi Hage wrote of "the inner world of the self and outer self of the world."[32] This duality is alive in Darwish, who holds self and not-self through language, which must serve as the homeland for both: "By the full power of my language," he writes, "I am the stranger."[33] Throughout *Mural*, surfaces—a sheet of paper for a poem, or the separation wall bearing a mural—are entrusted with both absence and presence. The images laid upon the wall must speak for the poet, creating a work of "sounding painting and silent poetry."[34] The separation wall holds the mural; his approaching death holds his expanding life; the attempt to erase his country, Palestine, inscribes it ever more deeply; and a name, temporarily given, remains with us all our lives. "One day," Darwish writes, "I will be a bird and will snatch my being out of my nothingness."[35]

In the last pages of *Mural*, another musicality emerges. Darwish takes the five Arabic letters that spell his name, Mahmoud, and scatters them through a single page of the poem. Darwish, writes Palestinian scholar Wafa' Saleh, repeats and resounds these letters, creating an echoing sonority which generates some thirty-four alliterations within eleven lines. The reverberation of these sounds, م’, ح’, م’, و’, د’ (mim, ha, mim, waw, dal) echo "upon the hearer of the dissected name."[36]

In his 2002 translation of the poem, Akash, who worked closely with Darwish during his life, omitted these eleven lines. They must have seemed untranslatable. Nearly a decade after Darwish's passing, Rema Hammami and John Berger offered another translation of *Mural*. Here is their translation of those eleven lines:

And my name mispronounced with its five
horizontal letters
My name . . . is mine.
mim / of lovesickness of the orphan of those who
complete the past
ha / of the garden and love, of two muddles and two losses
mim / of the rake of the lovesick of the exile prepared for
a death foretold
waw / of farewells of the central flower of fidelity to birth
wherever it may be and of a parent's promise
dal / of the guide of the path of tears of a studied galaxy
and a sparrow who cajoles me and makes me bleed
This name is mine

What becomes of a name dispersed in this way, or of a life scattered over existence? Darwish writes, "The transparent one within you is your ode." He says, "Green, the land of my poem is green." His conversation with his name, and with the temporary possession of a name, spanned a lifetime. In "The Owl's Night," he writes, "Perhaps I can handle my life here. Perhaps I can now give birth to myself and choose different letters for my name / Perhaps I will be transformed within my name."[37] Two years before his death, he completed a final long work, *Fī Ḥaḍrat al-Ghiyāb.* Translated by Sinan Antoon as *In the Presence of Absence,* its first line reads, "I scatter you before me line by line with a mastery I possessed only in beginnings."[38]

In reimagining *Mural,* the translators had to discover what could be saved or omitted or relinquished, what cannot be excised from the mural of existence, and what is present in its absence. In every transformation, something is left by the wayside; there is no alternative. Hammami and Berger retain those lines; Akash excises them, and yet his translation of *Mural* is of a different order. Akash's *Mural* has an unstable genius, a radiant fullness. But even this extraordinary effort will not capture what an Arabic language reader and listener perceives, or what a Palestinian feels, as they read and reread *Mural* in its original language or hear the poem in recordings of Darwish's own voice.[39]

Should we think of this as a loss? I feel it is something altogether different from loss, part of the living and alchemical quality of a work of art. Such creations, extremely rare, make us fall quiet. Quiet is not only, or not always, the absence of sound but a stillness which makes a reality of hearing. Within this hearing there is also the awareness of our limitations. Nearly all of the living world operates in ranges which human eyes and ears cannot perceive. What we hear at the very limits of our senses is precious. This recognition of loss stirs each of us into movement. In *Mural,* a man writes his own eulogy, and the eulogy for all who must make this journey into namelessness. We make this journey knowing that the very depths of our longings must go unfulfilled.

Help me, the poem says, to bear my survival.[40]

"What have you done there in the earthly world," the poem asks.[41]

The poem answers, "What wind brought you here? Tell me the name of your wound, and I will know the roads where we might twice become lost."[42]

Derived from *muralis,* or wall, we have the word *mural.* The wall is a separation barrier, while the mural seeks to transform the horizon, to be a painting which extends sight. "So let us then go," Darwish says, "to the highest mural."[43]

In the depth of the night, when our streets and avenues no longer ring with human noise, when the midnight shifts of the world begin, the flowers which grow in response to moonlight bloom. Our sight becomes monochromatic, the outlines of things blur, and gradations of sound help us trace the darkness. We know that sheets of rain and newly fallen snow orchestrate distinct sensory worlds, and that the feeling of a dry, windless darkness opens its own texture of quiet. What we say to one another at night and what we say to one in the day are different.

Nights persist in our memories distinct from days. The nights have something eternal in them. I remember walking out of Vancouver General Hospital, after ten days at the bedside of a beloved friend. She passed away in the night, holding the hands of her family, and afterwards I walked through the darkness feeling at sea and broken and desperate with love. I was grateful for the night which hid me from myself. I remember summer nights when, sleepless, I sat at a window in Shanghai, drifting. I remember bicycling home in the dark, after watching a red moon emerge in a Berlin sky. The night makes me quiet but not speechless. At the limits of my senses, my questions open.

In the night I wake in a sweat, open my phone, and see images of the destruction of Gaza. I see the bombings and killings of the night. Paramedics, children, teachers, mothers and fathers, families. I wake to see a headline that two hundred thousand Palestinians have been killed or injured in Gaza, a number confirmed by the former chief of staff of the Israeli forces, who says, "We took the gloves off from the first minute."[44] This touch, I think. This touch we lay upon one another. This touch in the hours of the night. Nearly every night for 734 days, aerial attacks, bombs and drones have annihilated the lives of Palestinians.

Opportunists, wrote John Berger, fragment the world. "Disasters are flowing together into a delta that has no name. . . . Nothing to do today but to try to walk on the bitter waters of this nameless delta."[45]

But how to walk on these bitter waters? Again and again, the night is the backdrop for our spectacle of man-made suns, exploding stars and limitless death. We see men and women using the light of their cellular phones to search for their beloved, their world. We see children burning to death before our eyes. The word *awe* stems from *agis,* fear and anguish, and from the root word *ail,* or *ailen,* to afflict. Awe became our word for fright, terror and, eventually, reverence. Once we used it for the trembling we felt before God, and now we use it for the mass deaths we inflict on those powerless to escape the euphoria of our killing.

Simone Weil writes that Homer, in recounting the Trojan War in the *Iliad,* warned his listeners that force is always on loan from fate and that no one is spared, and eventually even the victors are forced to bow their necks to force. Homer does not pretend otherwise, she says, does not veil reality, does not disguise the obscenity of killing, does not transform it with meaning. But there are certain things, Weil continues, which Homer does wrap in poetry. Those things which war threatens, those things that killing destroys and degrades, those sacred things that war reviles and makes meaningless, she writes, the *Iliad* wraps in poetry.

To wrap the things that matter in poetry, to make a shroud for what hatred destroys and degrades, century after century, it is the task, perhaps the only task, of the writer, it is necessary, and it is not enough.

With every round of slaughter, the profiteers increase their wealth. And who, these profiteers ask, is not complicit? Who, they ask, does not partake in the capital of the world, who among us has clean hands? They say we are complicit when we speak and we are complicit when we say nothing. They say that words of literature and poetry salvage the past in order to give it a new burial.

I feel speechless. The poets know that language is a living thing and a collective possession. The executioners take language for themselves and have mastered its use.

"What art does," writes Omar El Akkad, "is meet us at the site of our insanity, our derangement, the plainly irrational mechanics of what it means to be human. There comes from this, then, at least a working definition of a soul: one's capacity to sit with the mysteries of a thing that cannot in any rational way be understood—only felt, only moved through. And sometimes that thing is so grotesque—what we do to one another is so grotesque—that sitting with it feels an affront to the notion of art as a conduit of beauty."[46]

"I have found that the land is fragile," writes Darwish, "and the sea, light; I have learned that language and metaphor are not enough to restore place to a place."[47]

When I slip the microcassette into the machine, it does not break. The machine functions, the cassette plays, and voices begin to sound, one following the next. There are dozens of messages for my roommates and for myself. At different times, each of our mothers calls. There are messages about potluck dinners, jobs, groceries. Messages from ex-boyfriends, colleagues, lost friends. And then my sister's voice, crying. She says, *Please call me right away. Please call me right away.* And yet more messages.

In the stopping and starting of the tape, some voices are interrupted, some are cut short. A later day is recorded over a previous week, but then an earlier day surfaces, so that the voices and days interlace.

Hi maddie, it's mom. I . . . I don't know where you are but I thought we were supposed to go have lunch and then go to the other place. So give me a call if you can't make it. It's 604-880-6818. Again, it's 604-880-6818. Thanks, bye.

The tape continues. There is a message from my roommate's mom, who says that it is 9:25 in the evening on Tuesday the nineteenth of November. There is a message about a reading at the local library. The beep of the answering machine, dividing each message, is high-pitched and flat and familiar. And then:

Hi, this is a message for Madeleine Thien. Hi maddie, it's mom. Just to . . . let me know when I can pick those up. I can pick it up tomorrow night if you like. I'll be in the office tomorrow but I'll be in a meeting all day. But you can reach me at home tonight. So, take care, bye.

My mother's voice is warm and soft. When I hear her, I feel as if I have been swept back into her presence. I hear now what I did not hear at the time. The failure of her heart that had already been set in motion, the pneumonia settling in her lungs. She sounds so incredibly tired. I hear, too, the joy of the everyday. Plans to meet, errands to run, dinners on the horizon. My mother arriving in her car, that car in which we shared so many conversations and songs. I miss you, I think. I miss you and I miss you.

I listen to both sides of the tape and then I remove the microcassette, return it to its plastic case, and weep.

Late that night, my cousin in Vancouver sends me photos of his newborn son. Mother and child are beautiful. My cousin tells me that the baby was born on the anniversary of my aunt's death twenty-three years ago.

He was born on this day, my cousin says, the first day of all the days to come.

"One day," writes Mahmoud Darwish in *Mural*, "I will be what I want to be."

These words echo four times in the poem, and each repetition is followed by a different image.

"One day, I will be a bird and will snatch my being out of my nothingness."

"One day, I will be a poet."

"One day, I will be a grapevine."

"One day, I will be a thought that no sword nor any book will bear to the wasteland."

This last variation, which appears first, takes root in me and cannot be pulled loose.

I ask my beloved what this line might mean.

He says, It is a thought that has no instrument or tool to carry it. A thought that is not written in stone, that belongs to no creed and no holy book. A thought that cannot be used as propaganda or as an instrument for violence.

It is a thought, my beloved says, that can only come from being in the world.

Today, a writer named Muhammad al-Zaqzouq, who has an invitation to France through a program that offers refuge to scholars and artists, and who has managed to obtain all the correct paperwork, and who, through donations, has satisfied all the financial requirements for himself, his wife, Ula, and their three small sons, is trapped in Palestine. Despite the efforts of the French government, Palestinians have not been permitted by the occupying power to evacuate. Al-Zaqzouq has tried to write over the past two years. He has written about the destruction of the apartment that was his children's home, about their continuous displacement, and about hunger. In the morning, the adults and the three little boys, aged seven, five and three, share some biscuits, and then there is nothing more to eat until the evening when they share tea.

One day, he writes, he manages to buy an exorbitantly expensive sack of looted flour. He carries home this "priceless treasure," which brings a "dark joy amid the wasteland of fear and grief." He and Ula make dough from the flour, and shape the dough into thin rounds, but they do not have an oven to bake the bread. Fortunately, he continues, mud ovens, used by rural Gazan families for cooking and baking, can be found between the buildings. The families ask only that others bring enough paper or cardboard for fuel. But al-Zaqzouq has none. All he has to burn are books. "It had never occurred to me," he writes, "that I might one day have to weigh a book against a piece of bread for my children." These books, he continues, included:

> works on philosophy, society and religion, novels, and poetry collections gifted to me by friends at their book signings, with dedications hand-written in the front pages. The books felt to me like part of a shared memory belonging to all those people, some of whom were still in Gaza, some of whom had gone abroad, and some of whom had died while searching for life. The more I thought about it, the clearer the feeling burned: my library was a pulsing bundle of flesh and blood and memories and lives and errands run in Gaza's streets and alleys and evenings spent in cafes and on the seafront in summer and in winter.

He tells himself he cannot burn a single page of a book, and that there must be some other answer. He goes outside to search.

> But as I walked down the street, there wasn't a scrap of paper or cardboard to be seen. People had used up everything they could find in the garbage containers, and as I searched, I realized others were searching with me. Young and old alike were raking the ground with their eyes, all looking for paper to give to the village women so as to bake their bread. I wondered for a second if there might be none to be found anywhere in Hamad City, and I was overcome by a crushing sense of despair as I looked left

and right, running now, chasing the paper mirage. I nearly went back to the flat and took two books from the shelves, and would have burned them to bake bread for the hungry children had not the owner of the store beneath our building intervened. He seemed to have been watching me on my search, and had finally decided to help me when he saw I was losing hope.

"You're looking for cardboard boxes, aren't you?" he asked. "Do you have any?" I replied eagerly. "Here," he said, handing me three large pieces of cardboard. "Nothing's too precious for you." I thanked him several times before racing back upstairs, happy and proud, and grateful to the man for rescuing me from the sea of regret I'd soon have been drowning in had I begun to burn my library.

They were only a small and humble collection of books, but to me they were the souls of the people who'd written them—and this was no metaphor or poetic image, but a truth I had felt for many years.[48]

"One day, I will be a thought that no sword nor any book will bear to the wasteland." I ask myself and I ask this world what these words, born of being here together, could mean.

MADELEINE THIEN

"The executioners take language for themselves and have mastered its use. The poets know that language is a living thing and a collective possession."

"Improvisation isn't a refusal of the structure but the addition of new architectures—of care, resistance, indeterminacy and listening. It is the ongoing rehearsal of an alternative mode of existing, working together."

IMMANUEL WILKINS

The Red Record

IMMANUEL WILKINS

Improvisation is a complex system that absorbs everything around it. To improvise in performance is to be like water, willing to pivot at any moment or take on a new shape. An improviser feeds off balance and imbalance, creating momentum and motion that sends signals reverberating out. There are no expectations, just an availability—a willingness to be present. Every moment is informed by a host of small calculations moving so quickly that they register as intuition. As Cecil Taylor reminds us, "Each moment presents not the possibility, but the necessity of everything being new."[1] The improviser's task is not only to respond but to continually reconstitute the terms of engagement. Their job is to be as open and relaxed as possible in the moment of reception, with acute awareness and a heightened emotional sensitivity. Improvising is a vulnerable place to exist in, embracing a radical acceptance of every event that occurs in the music. The veil of the artist has to be lifted, and the emotional intensity ever present. Yet the pressure of that intensity lies in a small, powerful, liminal space of restraint. As the practice becomes more rigorous, the work begins to break the walls of performance, extending into a spiritual environment in which the soloist exists in a space beyond all logical form. This is what jazz musicians call the "big room." It is the moment the music is freed from its form and the structure becomes subjective. This is a meditation zone of nothingness, where the musician becomes a vessel and a channel.

In jazz music, when someone plays a note or a series of notes that don't belong to the corresponding chord, it is called playing "outside" or "going out." To play "out" means to go against or abandon the preexisting harmonic structures and build your own language. When I first began improvising, I was interested in how certain musicians would negotiate the "outness" or how they would get to the outside. Some musicians had devices and internal logics that they would employ in order to get out, and for other musicians, it would remain a mystery to me. Naturally, playing out is a way to create harmonic tension and release—you go away and you come back home. For a radical improviser, one can stay out for a whole solo. I was in love with the friction between the inside of the accompaniment and the outside of the improviser. The proximity created a whole new feeling. I went on to desire the complete outside—where there is no inside. I fell in love with the avant-garde. The avant-garde is the front line; it is the danger zone. In this sound, all of the textural properties are freed up to press up against one another at any given moment. There is freedom and no explicit preconceived material to adhere to, but there is a language that one has to know the vernacular of. Each member of the ensemble is creating forms, systems and structures that carry meanings and invitations unbounded by normative ideas of western melody, harmony, rhythm or form. The friction of outness is the escape relational to that which is always on you.

I want to explore the friction of outness through the blues. The blues scale is derived from the pentatonic scale. The pentatonic is a five-note scale that comprises the tonic or root note, the 2nd interval, the 3rd interval, the 5th interval and the 6th interval. The pentatonic scale is one of the most widely used across all of music, both eastern and western. The blues scale introduces a sixth note, the tritone. This note is a break, a rupture, it is a note that bears absolutely no relation to the key at all; in fact, it is the farthest note in relation to the root. The tritone bears no gravitational pull in relation to the root. Balancing perfectly in its alienation, it sustains the tension and is a refusal to the resolution. This note is often called the "blue note." The blues introduced a friction and a complexity in the sound that was alien. The blues is the funk, the ferment—an element that shocks the system. The blues was birthed in the outdoors. Plantation songs were sent up straight into the open air; the blues carried the pain and the pleasure. The sonic world of the work song is bound up with the sublime and the grotesque. The sonic hybrid carries codes—the very codes that are contained in Aunt Hester's scream, according to Fredrick Douglass.[2] This complex coding of sound is how the jazz musician is able to continuously remix the sonic language and prevent the theft of the improvised form, continuously changing the parameters and systems of what you hear. Playing the "out" notes was the way to free up the sound. To play outside the chord structure is to enter the realm of the unknown, where every note becomes a possibility and the music begins to feel boundless. Outness allows you to self-individuate—to create your own internal logic.

Charlie Parker and John Coltrane would create their own sets of chord changes that they would then superimpose over a piece of music. These chord structures were spectral-chromatic forms that would push against the preexisting harmony, allowing them to navigate the outside using their own logical basis. I began searching for my own process of building a harmonic system—the purpose being simply to find creative ways of getting from point A to point B. My system is less focused on the chords' relationship to the preexisting harmony, but more related to the intervals that make up a chord. This system I've created for myself involves shifting intervals that correspond to a triad stepwise to freely voice-lead atonally. These shifting triads can be improvised with, abstracting the triad itself and leading to an angular melodic form that obscures its own logic. I'm interested in working with, and reworking, basic fundamental units. These progressions in modern music aren't just about more complexity within predefined parameters but, rather, consistently redefining the parameters. Ornette Coleman said in a 1996 interview, "The notes are the same, but your brain is constantly defining what these notes are recalling to you."[3] My harmonic approach is coming out of an unfinished theory of Coleman's he called "Harmolodics." He was working on a theory book that he wasn't able to finish in his lifetime. I was drawn to the idea of developing an improvised melodic idea to its completion, beyond its relationship to the tonal center—following the line through, versus editing the line to fit within the corresponding harmony. As an improviser's notes in a phrase venture farther outside the structure, the notes begin to carry a different meaning, the frequencies begin to vibrate differently, and the environment around the note shifts.

I want to trace the figurative musical outside through to the literal. Saxophonist Sonny Rollins took a hiatus from performance and secretly began practicing on the Williamsburg Bridge almost daily between 1959 and 1961, playing up to sixteen hours per day. Playing an instrument outside teaches you about sound. Musicians need to hear what the sound is like with no walls, where the sound goes out and disappears, never coming back to you. I have a Fluxus-style piece I call "BLACK MUSIC." Step one is to go into the forest away from any and every potential of capture; step two is to play as many notes out into the world as you desire. I wonder if Blackness is simply vanishing into obscurity with no record, bearing no trace, and no account for existing. In *Lose Your Mother*, Saidiya Hartman refers to enslaved Africans in the hold as "those who had left no record of their lives."[4] I am interested in the tension between this violence of erasure and that condition as a possibility, an aesthetic or ontological space outside of the capture. Maybe *Black* and *outside* are one and the same: to be "in the black" is to be in the clear—it is boundlessness, the beyond, endless possibility; it's what Sun Ra was looking for in the cosmos.

Black space, the beyond, the unknown, is a place of clarity. It is an eternal space that we visit like an altar. It is an opening and clearing through which light flows. Throughout my conceptual and compositional practice, I have engaged with the notion of the vessel as both a musical and metaphysical condition. I composed *The 7th Hand* in 2022, which is a seven-movement suite that's an inquiry into spirit possession articulated through a progressive dissolution of composed material into improvised material. It was an experiment using performance to reach a state of witness—an aspirational state in which we no longer are the ones making the music.

Structurally, the suite unfolds across seven movements, beginning with the most composed material and gradually moving toward the seventh movement, which contains only a single notated pitch. Each movement modulates metrically by a triplet subdivision, descending toward the central fourth movement before ascending once more. The final movement functions as a free improvisation, a culmination of the energy of every piece prior, demanding that the performer fully inhabit the state of the vessel. Devices such as repetition, modality, chant and free improvisation—sonic and/or ritual technologies that recur across spiritual practices in the diaspora—operate as forms of invocation in the work. I wanted to exhaust musical materials and formal systems, where the boundaries of the performer and the score might dissolve. The complexity of the material demands an intimacy with the material. I have thought of this approach as a molecular rigor that extends into the quantum—an attention to the microstructures of improvisation, a process of layering and superimposition so detailed as to induce disorientation, an entry point into the subconscious.

The idea of the *vessel* continues to exert a persistent hold on my practice. I want to use performance as a vehicle to open up the body as a portal—womb. It is a site of passage, where histories known and unknown move through and are transformed in the process. In this sense, I'm thinking through the body's function as an *immaterial archive*, a living repository that music has the potential to awaken and breathe life into. I'm thinking about Fred Moten's notion of "the resistance of the object," where the black body, rendered as a commodity, evades capture through the sonic.[5] I then want to imagine improvised black music, within this framework, as a tool for fabulation—the improvisational encounter is a speculative mode of historical recovery, bathing in the sound, mining the ruins. I'm interested in the ancestors I can hear through the horn, or through the rhythm of our collective notes. I want to retrace the histories lost to the Atlantic, those that persist in the interstices of memory and the imagination. The sonic, in its abstraction, opens a field of possibility. Resonance, vibration or haunting. These hauntings, Avery Gordon terms them "ghostly matters,"[6] emerge as visitations from the *afterlives of the archive*. Improvisation functions as both an epistemological and ancestral technology, where the performer is in negotiation with that which exceeds the self. The body, or vessel, is the archive and the instrument. Music is the heirloom—an inheritance that continues to code and recode itself, creating these new maps left in our traces.

I want to continue to think about the vessel in performance through another project of mine entitled *Blues Blood*, which is a piece composed for saxophone, piano, bass, drums, three vocalists, and a chef cooking onstage. In addition to the musicians, the chef is miked up. The sound of food preparation figures within the sonic framework throughout the piece, with smells emanating into the room moments in. The meal is then shared with audience members when the show is over. The title comes from a quote from Daniel Hamm, who was a part of the Harlem Six—a group of young boys falsely accused of murder during the Little Fruit Stand Riot in 1964. He described seeking medical attention for his wounds in jail, saying, "I had to, like, open the bruise up and let some of the blues [bruise] blood come out to show them." I was attracted to the slip of the tongue—"blues" instead of "bruise." I began to think about the blues as this kind of "pleasure in pain," a willingness to wallow in the grief or steep in the sorrow, yet the blues is something that feels so good. Blood has been a symbol for all things generational and ancestral. The phrase "Blues Blood" called me to think about the archive—what has been left for us, and what we will leave behind. The project engages with what survives despite historical violence—the traces, or affective intensities, that constitute an archive beyond the normative document. The archive here is what has been preserved, but also what has been transmitted, through performance, through the body, through food or through sound. This archive holds work that cannot be stolen.

The pieces feature long sections of free improvisation in which any of the three vocalists or four musicians can spontaneously compose. I began composing for this project from two haikus Theaster Gates wrote and allowed me to set to music. This text became the catalyst for the piece "Matte Glaze," the first song of the suite. The text for me is both about a pot and about the body. The haiku says: "Luster on my skin . . ." "inside this vessel / lawd, build me a home dwelling. . . ." I believe that the voice is like the eyes—you can hear into the soul. With the voice, the veil is removed. I wanted to be able to use text sculpturally in the piece, allowing the lyrics to be as abstract as the notes, and I desired to write for the vocalists that I heard in my mind. When I compose at the piano, I sing the melody line in falsetto to replicate my saxophone. In a way I have been chasing the sound of the voice on the horn. In the compositional process for *Blues Blood*, I began studying the vocalists' individual practices and strived to make music that I would imagine they would make for themselves. I wanted them to feel like they were creating in a familiar universe—or better yet, their universe. My compositional function was to be the glue, the through line between all of these different voices. I wanted to create the conditions for encounter. Like the seating chart for a great dinner. I wanted to project certain proximal outcomes in the way I composed for each individual and the collective. The voice isn't fit for as many intervalic acrobatics as an instrument, so I was challenged with keeping the melodies in specific ranges and being intentional with angularity. When writing this body of work, I was constantly asking myself, "Is this enough music?" Writing with the intention of leaving room for a large amount of free improvisation felt scary for me. I was afraid my musical invocations would not have the momentum to carry us through. The process of writing for this group was an exercise of trust. I left a lot in the hands of the ensemble. The song structures morphed and molded differently each time we performed the music. The less intervention I make as a composer, the more agency the player has. The space in the music is what gives the composed material life. These are moments in the music we call on ancestors, pray together, exercise acts of care and receive sustenance.

I thought about food as another form that draws on cultural heirlooms. There are so many recipes and traditions passed down from generation to generation through oral tradition around the kitchen or dinner table. As we perform the piece, the room begins to fill with smells that transport you to the living room. At the dinner table, sharing a meal with friends or family, I often find myself asking, "Did you have enough?" The sharing of food becomes a practice of care in the everyday. This is a mirror to the bandstand—the music's open sections are a buffet of sorts, with the musicians equally dividing the portions amongst themselves. *Blues Blood*'s sensory experience disarms both the performer and the audience member, creating a space that feels both alien and deeply familiar.

Across both of my longform through-composed works, I've explored the possibilities of the body as a vessel—in *The 7th Hand*, through the lens of spirit possession, and in *Blues Blood*, through the lens of ancestral knowledge. I'm seeking a form of witness in performance, an out-of-body experience in which you are a witness to the work that is being done through you. In my practice, I've engaged with the role of the accompanist, existing in service of the thing, versus to be the thing. My role is the channel. It allows me to exalt the music and to be humble in the face of it. My relationship to the ensemble is one of vulnerability, surrender and embrace.

While improvising, you are creating melodic material, thematic material, rhythmic material, phrases with symmetry, asymmetry, following laws of balance and imbalance, all while listening to one another. This listening is an active internalization of everything going on around you, in what may be a geospatial sense; what you offer is then both in response and in resistance. So much improvised information is being offered by every instrument at any given second that each musician has to choose what material to react to. It is a constant negotiation and an assessment of intention. Fred Moten suggests that "improvisation is the always already performance of the sociality that makes it possible."[7] There is no singular black genius in the music, and the "solo" is a rehearsal of collectivity. Each decision on the bandstand carries an intention, an indication of where the music can move. These considerations are microscopic and feel like kinetic gears continuously morphing, giving way to new shapes and forms. McCoy Tyner talks about his time with the John Coltrane quartet, saying, "It was like we were four pistons in an engine." It is a symbiotic relation that performs a critical lens inherently nonbinary in nature.

On the bandstand, we travel beyond aesthetics, beyond the binary notions of good and bad—we are just making, just being, we are lost in it, not at all occupied with giving folk a good show. In collaboration with the same three instrumentalists for eight years, we have reached a point in which public failure is always imminent. The music is borne into a place of risk—true risk for us is to venture into the unknown, wherein lies the highest reward and the greatest failure. Sylvia Wynter would call for an aesthetic no longer bound to the colonial order of representation, judgment or mastery.[8] Or as my friend, South African pianist Nduduzo Makhatini, has said, "The performance is an ongoing rehearsal." The work is all process, excess, labor. "Practice" is the escape route for me as a musician. What I love about listening to John Coltrane is that it sounds like he's constantly reworking and rethinking the material on the bandstand. The performance is now the practice—or the process. This is the secret and the sacred, made public. A part of me doesn't believe we should be listening to these moments, out of the sheer intensity and resonant power these moments hold. The process that I am getting at is not a state of underdevelopment. It is where you begin to see the light, where the intensity is high and the labor begins to yield this certain type of beauty.

The audience is now listening in on the intimacy of working it out, of incompleteness, of ante-performance or anti-performance. It feels like a sacrifice, with both logistical and physical undertones, or spiritual ones. I often wonder how much the John Coltrane Quartet considered the audience. I want to believe that in order to transcend, one has to do so without the gaze of the outside. To "practice" in performance means to escape whatever is on you; it's a refusal of the conditions expected of your production. I want to imagine the intimacy of the practice room as a heightened spiritual state, or one of Zen focus. Spending prolonged periods in this state, you arrive at a feeling in which the excess of rigor is disorienting. It is a threshold where the accumulation of connections and associations begins to collapse the coherence of meaning itself. It is what lies beyond aesthetics. It is a spiritual modality that sits outside the normative realm of meaning. It is a sublime state that is after knowing.

Practice, as in the work you do in preparation for live performance, for an improviser, is interesting because it involves working things out without a certain set of key variables. Certain things can develop only through playing with the ensemble. Overall, there are not many ways to replicate the conditions of your stamina while practicing. There is a slow physical fatigue that sets in over a seventy-five- to ninety-minute set, and you have to account for how to create in ways that obscure or highlight that fatigue. When the physical fatigue sets in, the inhibitions lower and the playing becomes unconscious. Reaction time is a great gauge of how intensely focused and in tune I am with the ensemble at a given moment. When the ensemble hasn't played together for a while, the reaction time is slower. Being able to internalize and evaluate material quickly, phrase and flow effortlessly, or turn corners quickly, is predicated upon the trust but also the time spent with other members in performance. There's an agility that an ensemble can have when we visit the altar every day, when we are in constant communion with one another. We become a body, a unit, an organism that amorphously moves and takes on a new shape in each moment. The telepathy that comes with this flow state is bound up with the finality of declaration that only exists in performance, not in practice. Everything is to be questioned in the practice room, and there's a humility I have in that space that is no longer present when I reach the stage. On the stage, I forget about all of the things I'm practicing and I own the decisions I make. In the ensemble, we fall forward together.

I want to propose the notion that for myself and the group of musicians I have been working with, the music, as well as the ensemble, is the generation of theory. The work that is done through the bandstand tells us that improvisation *is* the study. If the body is a vessel, then improvisation is the process by which the vessel theorizes. The solo becomes an epistemological event. In working with my ensemble, we have drawn on the work of the Association for the Advancement of Creative Musicians (AACM) for inspiration, as much as to have the honor of Roscoe Mitchell composing an original commission for us. In engaging with the framework of the ensemble, I look to George Lewis, who, in *A Power Stronger Than Itself: The AACM and American Experimental Music* (2008), frames the AACM as a site for Black experimental thought. I want to think alongside the text, asserting that music itself is a form of intellectual labor, and that Black music is Black study. George Lewis said, "The AACM's project was the elaboration of new models of community, autonomy, and imagination."[9] Black music is bound up with the sociality and collectivity of improvisation. There is no singular genius. It is relational to the internal workings of the ensemble, and it is inherently experimental in response to the grand experiment performed against Black people. The roles of the ensemble are constantly challenged and undercut, creating a language of community that shifts in responsibility, care, holding, intensity.

For my solo improvisational work, I've created graphic scores that function as musical instruction and/or transcription. These graphic scores attempt to extend improvisational language into material, charting and graphing the sound. I've thought of Tina Campt's *Listening to Images*,[10] in the attunement to the "haptic." Each work is a gestural transcription of saxophone improvisations, made in real-time response. The score is both the precursor to the performance and the excess of performance. These graphic scores attempt to render the spectrum and complexity of black music, challenging notions of legibility through the fugitive technologies of improvisation—coded material that takes on new shape and form every time. The work attempts to harness improvisation as a site of the Black experimental thought George Lewis proposes, as the work isn't about applied theory, but the doing, as theory. The scores exist as both visual works and musical propositions.

I began working on these pieces in 2023 after a friend and collaborator of mine, singer Yaw Agyeman, had described a style of improvising I do as "scribbling on the saxophone." I thought about the work of Butch Morris, who was a composer that developed a system called "conduction." This was a compositional technique that harnesses free improvisation through cues and gestures, sitting at an intersection between conducting, improvising and composing. I first encountered this experimental framework in a high school workshop in 2012, in which J.A. Deane, a close collaborator of Butch Morris, came to Philadelphia to teach a masterclass. I would then go on to play in ensembles conducted by Tyshawn Sorey that gave me more experience and insight into the techniques of conduction. The process opened my eyes to the possibilities of the ensemble as a collective instrument that could render a type of visuality. The conductor was able to sonically paint with the baton, creating textural rubs that were filled with the agency and self-determination of each improviser. In my visual practice now, I apply some of these conductive gestures onto works on paper, using them as disruptions to the musical staff, or as alternative pathways a soloist could take based on the preexisting structure of a song. In jazz music, the score is not set. It is a suggestion of a direction that a song can head in; that suggestion can be as detailed or as vague as the composer would like. I wanted my graphic scores to have a light touch—a visual proposition that would give traces of an idea, a direction, a zone in which the soloist could generate material.

One of the biggest mysteries of Black music is how to notate it. There's no way to calculate James Jamerson's basslines, Clyde Stubblefield's high-hat or Jimmy Lyons's saxophone sound. "Song X" by Ornette Coleman exists in a realm beyond the limits of a score. What makes Black music sound Black is the space in between the rhythms, the space in between the notes, the notes that sit in the middle of two pitches, the bending, breaking and tearing of the sound. Notation doesn't account for the elements the immaterial has no language for. You can't learn black music out of a textbook, and you can't read black music off a sheet. You have to listen and listen until you learn how to access the feeling. Black music is of fugitive resonance and the notation should capture the feeling—one could argue the notes don't matter, anyway. The western system of notation doesn't have the capacity to hold the sound of Black music, and I look to abstraction and the critical imaginary as the only way of rendering the affects of the sonic.

A central component of study for an improviser is transcription. That entails a form of deep listening—listening to someone's improvisation, then, on the instrument, learning by ear every note, rhythm and articulation until one can replicate the solo. It is an opportunity to interact with the archive in a physical way, embodying the intuition of another improviser. In a broader sense, the purpose of transcription is not the replication of melodic material, but to understand the logics in which they created it. Some people choose to write these transcriptions out, and some memorize them from the recording. No matter how exacting one's study, the act of replaying an improvised solo can never replicate the temporality or affective charge of the initial.

In the 1920s, when jazz was still situated within a social field of dance, soloists would often play the same improvisations from the recording. The audience would sometimes know them and sing along. Though the notes and rhythms for the solo may be the same, the difference between the first iteration of the solo and its subsequent iterations remained palpable. There's a distinction between the spirit of immediacy and the reperformance of knowing. There is a breath and life that is limited in the performance of a transcription. It is important to note that to transcribe is to enter into a dialogue with the aftermath of a performance. My approach to the graphic score calls for a radical reinterpretation of that aftermath, one that leverages illegibility as a means to generate new material that arguably bears no index to the sonic offerings it is derived from.

In music making, we step into the zone of unknowing. The vessel holds the gestures both in excess and of proposition, a fragment of the theory that is performed through the body. The ensemble becomes an organism breathing together and constantly reshaping itself from within. Improvisation isn't a refusal of the structure but the addition of new architectures—of care, resistance, indeterminacy and listening. It is the ongoing rehearsal of an alternative mode of existing, working together. It is a meditation that allows the body into an archive for the unrecorded. Playing is remembering, imagining and refiguring the sonic as a site of the vessel. The vessel holds the sound as it lives inside its walls—it holds the echoes and traces.

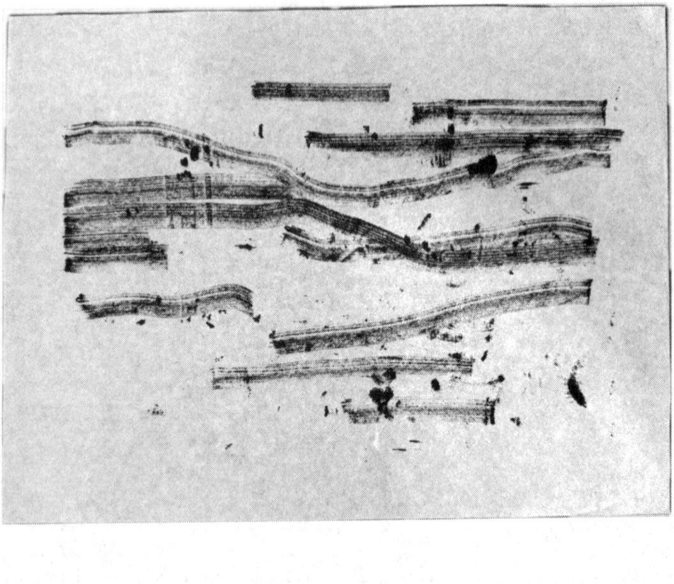

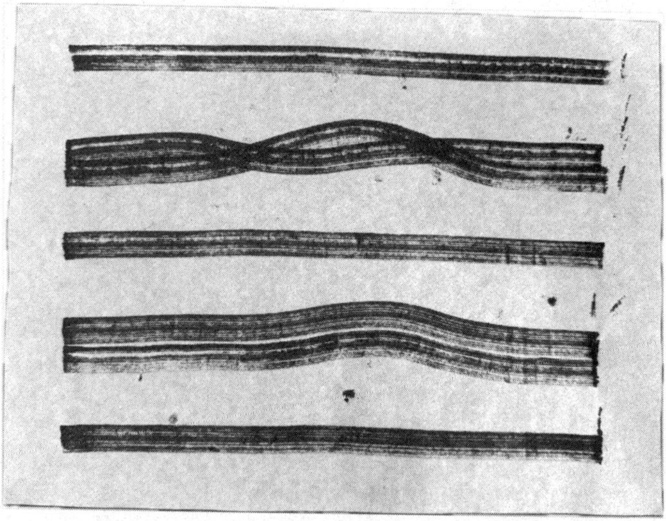

1.

Immanuel Wilkins
A
F(♯11)/A A5
D♭-7(add4)
C
A-9(add4)
E6
A♭-7(add4) D♭-7(add4)
B
B2/E
E-9(♯5)
GMaj7
D♭2
CΔ7(add6)
A-7

Closing Remarks

OLA MOHAMMED

Assalamu'alaikum. First, I want to thank Dr. Christina Sharpe for inviting me to be here. I'm deeply grateful for the opportunity to speak to the depth and scale of the work that this year's Alchemists offer us this evening—thinking with and through *Sound at the Interregnum*.

I take this time and space to riff on what the ensemble of Alchemists—Glen Coulthard, Canisia Lubrin, Madeleine Thien and Immanuel Wilkins—offer us. Each lecture unsettles the limits of the visual world, of words, of order, of time, of space, of scale. They use sound as method, offering other ways of knowing—of knowing terror, melancholy, beauty, refusal and invention.

Psychoacoustics tells us that sound is both a physical event and a perceptual one. Technically, as Dan Hosken explains,[1] sound is the sensation produced when our organs of hearing are stimulated by vibrations moving through air, water, land or other mediums. These vibrations—sound waves—emerge through the repeated pattern of compression and release: Air molecules are pushed together, then allowed to spring apart, then pressed together once again. This cyclical motion is what enables sound to travel. Thinking with this definition through Black and Indigenous studies, we can understand sound—both as material and metaphor—as inherently relational. Sound doesn't exist in isolation; it emerges through vibrations and contact, echoing Édouard Glissant's claim that "relation informs not simply the relayed but also the relative and the related."[2]

As Julian Henriques argues, "sound is always a dynamic event, forever incomplete and continually in a state of change."[3] Sound and sonic practices are multisensory, intimate and visceral. They refuse capture; they disrupt time and space to allow us to register *different ways of being.* Tonight's lectures work together in what I register as a four-part composition—Noisescape, Bridge, Quiet, Vessel—each carrying its own tone, its own register, and harmonizing a mutual terrain. This terrain insists we as audience, witness and ensemble consider the following questions: What does it mean to hear, listen and experience our relations to ourselves, to our communities, to the environment? How do practices of critical listening allow us to sense the urgency of sound at the interregnum?

We are called together by tonight's Alchemists to refuse what Dylan Robinson names "hungry listening." Instead, we experiment with ways of listening that are attuned to Black and Indigenous sovereignties, epistemologies, ontologies and practices that expose the violence and impossibility of a "neutral" listener, to amplify decolonial practices which the global majority have long used to unsettle and reshape the world.

Movement I: Noisescape

[play 10- to 15-second clip: Sudanese ululation and protests][4]

Glen Coulthard attunes us to the noisescapes of the Yellowknives Dene community following the discovery of gold. Coulthard attunes us to the sounds of violence, terror and dispossession that is central to colonial and imperial logics. Frantz Fanon tells us, "for in a very concrete way Europe has stuffed herself inordinately with the gold and raw materials of the colonial countries . . . the wealth which smothers her is that which was stolen from the underdeveloped peoples."[5] The noisescape of the Giant Mine reverberates transnationally across borders and time. It echoes in the UAE's imperial extractive practices and the violence of gold mining in Sudan, and in major global companies mining cobalt in Congo. The same greed that depleted the inconnu at the Yellowknife River, that poisoned the people and land, drives the global economic reliance on fossil fuels, intensifying the climate catastrophe and its destructive wake that we currently see in Hurricane Melissa ravaging Jamaica, Haiti, the Dominican Republic and Cuba.

Coulthard offers us noise as method to understand not only the acoustic/affective impact of colonialism—but also the material. And while the noisescape insists, we understand the violence of colonialism, and I extend to imperialism—Coulthard does not leave us *in* the violence. For Coulthard, "against this noise, drum songs work as counter-sonic forces. . . . Each beat of the drum insists that this land is not empty, not inert, not for the taking." The drums, the protest lyrics, the storm lead us to Movement II: Bridge.

Movement II: Bridge

[play 20-second clip: airport protest sounds, Grenada; drumming by Ahousaht Nation during destruction of residential school in BC][6]

> *In music, the bridge is often the part of a song that features new chord progressions, melodies and lyrics to break up the repetition of the verse and chorus structure. It is a departure that builds tension and new perspective.*

Canisia Lubrin's lecture, "A Catalogue of Bridges," channels the spirit of the definition of the musical bridge. She registers the Haitian Revolution, what Michel-Rolph Trouillot in *Silencing the Past* calls the "unthinkable revolution."[7] The Haitian Revolution disrupted the sociopolitical order of modernity. Like the bridge, the revolution built tension by recasting "The Slave" into an agentive figure who "made and unmade [the world]." Lubrin attunes us to the score of the long emancipation, where the work of dismantling the master's clock functions across time, space and scale. Rasheedah Phillips reminds us: "Western temporal norms privilege progress and futurity, often at the expense of cyclical, relational, and pluralistic understandings of time that are intrinsic to many Black and Indigenous cultures."[8]

Lubrin returns us to the stormy night of the Bois Kayiman ceremony, "the catalyst of the Haitian Revolution."[9] Bianca Beauchemin reminds us how through the events of the Bois Kayiman ceremony, "the land becomes a space of spiritual connection and resilience" (p. 79). The tremorous vibrations through drumming—the collective beating heart of the revolution, rupture the hold of domination. In these moments of rupture, we hear and feel new ways of being. From the drums of Bois Kayiman to the drums of Dene Nation, to the drums of Ahousaht Nation in Vancouver Island where a residential school is torn down, each stroke of the drum resounds the dispossessed's refusal to, as Lubrin puts it, "accep[t] oneself as the prisoner of history."

From the streets of Toronto where people rally against bubble zone bylaws, to the streets of Grenada where the people are refusing the implementation of US military equipment in Maurice Bishop airport, to the streets of Lima, Peru, where a state of emergency attempts to silence antigovernment protests, to the global sumud of freedom flotillas sailing to break the Israeli occupation's illegal siege on Gaza, the Catalogue of Bridges is a palimpsest, where the tremble of liberation refuses to capitulate to Fanon's "agents of government [who] speak the language of pure force,"[10] overturning the political and temporal logics and fault lines of modernity to guide us to new openings.

Movement III: Quiet

[no sound]

Madeleine Thien attunes us to the quiet in the lecture "'No Sword nor Any Book.'" Thien proclaims "quiet is not only, or not always, the absence of sound but a stillness which makes a reality of hearing." While much in this world remains undetectable—whether it be through the limits of translation, or the "ranges which human eyes and ears cannot perceive"—Thien reminds us that "what we hear at the very limits of our senses is precious." Thien's attentiveness to the quiet is akin to Christina Sharpe's wake work[11] and Aaron Joseph's mariner hospitality—"not pity, not policy. But the dignity of the undertow. A care that does not require reciprocity, legality, or name."[12]

To wait in the quiet insists we are attentive to and sit with loss, mourning and our longing. From noticing, like Thien, "the steady red light of the answering machine," to the loops of Khaled Nabhan's voice mourning the loss of his grandchildren, Tariq and Reem, ruh al-ruh—the soul of his soul that circulates social media and my mind—to Mahmoud Darwish's words, "one day, I will be a thought that no sword nor any book will bear to the wasteland,"[13] quietness at the interregnum serves as an invitation to attune ourselves to the absented presences that are not always visible, but are deeply resonant, felt and insist on movement.

Movement IV: Vessel

[play 15-second clip: D'Angelo][14]

Immanuel Wilkins's claim that "the improviser's task is not only to respond but to continually reconstitute the terms of engagement" draws us into the generative work of Black music / Black sound. His turn to the sixth note—the tritone, otherwise known as the "blue note"—registers dissonance not as failure. No, this dissonance, much like the break of the drumming of the Dene Nation, of Bois Kayiman, the vulnerability of sitting within the quiet is what Wilkins identifies as an opening, one that is a generative site.

I opened this movement with a calling from the track "Send It On" by D'Angelo, who recently passed away from a battle with pancreatic cancer, from his critically acclaimed album *Voodoo*. On October 19 and 20, Davie Studios Presents Listening Room held two jam sessions honoring the music of D'Angelo at the Longboat Hall, named after Tom Longboat, a famous Onondaga distance runner from the Six Nations of the Grand River. Entering the music hall that Sunday evening, witnessing the rotating ensemble of musicians move in and out of "the big room" on stage, sustaining the flow of improvisation, inviting us as audience to join the ensemble and, in Wilkins's words, "liste[n] in on the intimacy of working it out, of incompleteness, of ante-performance or anti-performance," was a night of Black study wherein we, the ensemble of performers and audience, theorized collectively. The Longboat Hall became the vessel—invoking histories of journeying and crossing both violent (the boat people of Haiti, of the Mediterranean) and transcendent (the groove).

In a 2014 interview with cultural writer Nelson George, D'Angelo stated that "blues was the nucleus of everything."[15] Blues is, as Wilkins reminds us, "an opening and clearing through which light flows. . . . It is what lies beyond aesthetics. It is a spiritual modality that sits outside the normative realm of meaning." From Wilkins's *7th Hand* and *Blues Blood* to D'Angelo's *Voodoo*, Black musicians become "a vessel and a channel" (per Wilkins) that help us, as D'Angelo sings, "send it up / send it through / send it back to you."

Thank you.

NOTES AND REFERENCES

Introduction

CHRISTINA SHARPE

NOTES

1. Dele Adeyemo, "Wey Dey Move," in *Borders, Human Itineraries and All Our Relation*, The Alchemy Lecture 1 (Alchemy by Knopf Canada, 2023), 7–41 (41).
2. See Dawoud Bey, *350,000*. I saw *350,000* in January 2024, where it was installed as part of the exhibition *Stony the Road*, Virginia Museum of Fine Arts in Richmond, Virginia.
3. Rebecca Belmore, "Wave Sound," https://www.rebeccabelmore.com/wave-sound/.
4. Laleh Khalili, "Breaking Bread Together," in *The City of Our Dreaming*, The Alchemy Lecture 2 (Alchemy by Knopf Canada, 2025), 70.
5. Anna Altman, "The Artist Who Captures the Sound of Political Terror," *New Yorker*, March 13, 2018, https://www.newyorker.com/culture/culture-desk/the-artist-who-captures-the-sound-of-political-terror.
6. Altman, "The Artist Who Captures the Sound."
7. Saidiya Hartman, *Wayward Lives, Beautiful Experiments: Intimate Histories of Social Upheaval* (W.W. Norton & Company, 2019), 232.
8. Shana L. Redmond, *Everything Man: The Form and Function of Paul Robeson* (Duke University Press, 2020), 24.
9. Redmond, *Everything Man*, 27.

10. Rich Smith, "Don Mee Choi's New Book, *Hardly War*, Is Challenging but Powerful Political Poetry," *Stranger*, March 2, 2016, https://www.thestranger.com/books/2016/03/02/23654617/don-mee-chois-new-book-hardly-war-is-challenging-but-powerful-political-poetry.
11. Tanya Tagaq, "Tongues" lyrics, "Tanya Tagaq montre les dents," *Le Devoir*, January 17, 2022, https://www.ledevoir.com/culture/musique/660996/entrevue-tanya-tagaq-montre-les-dents.
12. Tracy Chapman, "Talking About a Revolution" lyrics.

The Sounds of Extraction

GLEN SEAN COULTHARD

NOTES

1. Yellowknives Dene First Nation, *Weledeh Yellowknives Dene: A History* (YKDFN Elders Council, 1997).
2. John Sandlos and Arn Keeling, *The Price of Gold: Mining, Pollution, and Resistance in Yellowknife* (McGill-Queen's University Press, 2025), 11.
3. See Glen Sean Coulthard, "Palestinians and Native People Are Comrades: The Political Economy of Indigenous/Palestinian Solidarity," *Native American/Indigenous Studies* 12, no. 1 (2025); Glen Sean Coulthard, "Ayha's Prophecy: Uranium, Colonial Violence, and Dene Grounded Solidarity," *Funabulist* 60 (2025).
4. Sandlos and Keeling, *The Price of Gold*.
5. Trevor G. Reed, "Sonic Sovereignty: Performing Hopi Authority in Öngtupqa," *Journal of the Society for American Music* 13, no. 4 (2019), 510.
6. Sandlos and Keeling, *The Price of Gold*, 8.
7. Glen Sean Coulthard, *Red Skin, White Masks: Rejecting the Colonial Politics of Recognition* (University of Minnesota Press, 2014).

8. Julia Christensen and Rebecca Hall, "Welfare Colonialism and Resource Colonialism in Northern Canada," in *The Oxford Handbook of Social Policy in Canada*, ed. Daniel Béland, Rianne Mahon, and Alison Smith (online edition, Oxford Academic, 2025–), https://doi.org/10.1093/oxfordhb/9780197766859.013.0037.
9. Julia Christensen, *No Home in a Homeland: Indigenous Peoples and Homelessness in the Canadian North* (UBC Press, 2017).
10. Peter Ostergaard, "Quality of Life in a Northern City: A Social Geography of Yellowknife, NWT" (PhD diss., University of British Columbia, 1976).
11. Ostergaard, "Quality of Life in a Northern City."
12. Sandlos and Keeling, *The Price of Gold*, 26.
13. Sandlos and Keeling, *The Price of Gold*, 31.
14. See Coulthard, "Ayha's Prophecy."
15. Sandlos and Keeling, *The Price of Gold*, 34.
16. Quoted in Sandlos and Keeling, *The Price of Gold*, 34.
17. Sandlos and Keeling, *The Price of Gold*, 34.
18. Sandlos and Keeling, *The Price of Gold*, 21.
19. Caitlynn Beckett, "Beyond Remediation: Containing, Confronting and Caring for the Giant Mine Monster," *Environment and Planning E: Nature and Space* 4, no. 4 (2021): 1389.
20. Rebecca Hall and Brandon Pryce, "Colonial Continuities in Closure: Indigenous Mine Labour and the Canadian State," *Antipode* 56, no. 1 (2024): 102.
21. Hall and Pryce, "Colonial Continuities in Closure," 103.
22. Beckett, "Beyond Remediation."
23. Alia Al-Saji, "Touching the Wounds of Colonial Duration: Fanon's Anticolonial Critical Phenomenology," *Southern Journal of Philosophy* 62, no. 1 (2024): 2–23.
24. Rebecca Jane Hall, "Unsettling Extraction Through Community Relations to Land," in *Handbook on Politics and Society* (Edward Elgar Publishing, 2025), 76.
25. Leela Gilday, "Decoding Dene Music," *Up Here Magazine*, September 2020, https://uphere.ca/articles/decoding-dene-music.

26. Leanne Betasamosake Simpson, *As We Have Always Done: Indigenous Freedom Through Radical Resistance* (University of Minnesota Press, 2017).
27. Reed, "Sonic Sovereignty," 509.
28. Dylan Robinson, "Public Writing, Sovereign Reading: Indigenous Language Art in Public Space," *Art Journal* 76, no. 2 (2017): 85–99.
29. Reed, "Sonic Sovereignty."
30. Audra Simpson, "On Ethnographic Refusal: Indigeneity, 'Voice' and Colonial Citizenship," *Junctures: The Journal for Thematic Dialogue* 9 (2007).
31. Reed, "Sonic Sovereignty," 513.
32. Lauren Elizabeth Knight, "'Creator Gave Us Two Ears and One Mouth': Soundscapes as Signifiers of Environmental Crisis at the Intersections of Indigeneity and Acoustic Ecology," *Stream: Interdisciplinary Journal of Communication* 13, no. 1 (2021): 37–50.

A Catalogue of Bridges

CANISIA LUBRIN

WORKS CITED

Bennett-Coverley, Louise. (1982). "Dutty Tough." In *Selected Poems*. Sangster's Book Stores.

Brand, Dionne. (2001). *A Map to the Door of No Return: Notes to Belonging*. Doubleday Canada.

Brooks, Daphne A. (2021). *Liner Notes for the Revolution.*

Césaire, Aimé. (2001). *Notebook of a Return to the Native Land* (C. Eshleman & A. Smith, Trans. & Ed.). Wesleyan University Press. (Original work published 1939)

Césaire, A. (1983). *Cahier d'un retour au pays natal*. Présence Africaine.

Chery, Pierre Michel. (2010). "Douz Prensip Bois Kayiman: The Twelve Bois Kayiman Principles" (Emmanuel W. Védrine, Trans.). *Potomitan*. Web. https://www.potomitan.info/vedrine/bwa_kayiman.php

Coogler, R., Coogler, Z., Ohanian, S., Jordan, M. B. Steinfeld, H., Caton, M., O'Connell, J., Mosaku, W., Lawson, J., Miller, O. B., Guy, B., Lindo, D., Durald Arkapaw, A., Beachler, H., Shawver, M. P., Göransson, L., Carter, R. E., & Jones, A. (2025). *Sinners*. Warner Bros. Entertainment Inc.

Darwish, Mahmoud. (2007). "Silence for Gaza" (Sinan Antoon, Trans.). *Hayrat al-'A'id (The Returnee's Perplexity)*. Riyad al-Rayyis.

Daut, Marlene L. (2025). *The First and Last King of Haiti: The Rise and Fall of Henry Christophe*. Alfred A. Knopf.

Fanon, Frantz. (2008). *Black Skin, White Masks* (C. L. Markmann, Trans.). Grove Press. (Original work published 1952)

Gilmore, Ruth Wilson. (2015). *Organized Abandonment and Organized Violence: Devolution and the Police* [Video]. The Humanities Institute, UC Santa Cruz. https://vimeo.com/146450686

Glissant, Édouard. (1997). *Poetics of Relation* (B. Wing, Trans.). University of Michigan Press. (Original work published 1990)

Hartman, Saidiya V. (2019). *Wayward Lives, Beautiful Experiments: Intimate Histories of Social Upheaval*. W. W. Norton & Company.

Jackson, Michael. (1991). *Black or White* [Single]. Epic Records.

Jackson, Michael. (1995). *They Don't Really Care About Us* [Song]. In *HIStory: Past, Present and Future – Book I*. Epic Records.

James, C. L. R. (1989). *The Black Jacobins* (2nd ed.). Vintage Books.

Sharpe, Christina. (2010). *Monstrous Intimacies: Making Post-slavery Subjects*. Duke University Press.

Sparrow, Mighty. (1960). *Ten to One Is Murder* [Song]. On *Calypso Kings and Pink Gin*. RCA Records.

Trouillot, Michel-Rolph. (1995). *Silencing the Past: Power and the Production of History*. Beacon Press.

Walcott, Rinaldo. (2021). *The Long Emancipation*. Duke University Press.

Walcott, Rinaldo. (2023). *Towards Another Shape of This World*. In D. Adeyemo, N. Diaz, N. Y. Kisukidi, R. Walcott, & C. E. Sharpe (Eds.), *Borders, Human Itineraries, and All Our Relation* (pp. 11–22). Alchemy by Knopf.

No Sword nor Any Book

MADELEINE THIEN

NOTES

1. John Berger, *Here Is Where We Meet* (Pantheon Books, 2005), 6.
2. "Conscience," *Online Etymology Dictionary*, www.etymonline.com/word/conscience.
3. Adania Shibli, *Touch*, trans. Paula Haydar (Clockroot Books, 2010), 2.
4. Shibli, *Touch*, 13.
5. Shibli, *Touch*, 16.
6. Shibli, *Touch*, 18.
7. Shibli, *Touch*, 30, 18.
8. Shibli, *Touch*, 21.
9. Shibli, *Touch*, 38.
10. Shibli, *Touch*, 41, 45.
11. Shibli, *Touch*, 43.
12. Shibli, *Touch*, 43.
13. Shibli, *Touch*, 64.
14. Shibli, *Touch*, 68.
15. Gaston Bachelard, *The Poetics of Space*, trans. Maria Jolas (Penguin Books, 2014), 8.
16. Shibli, *Touch*, 72.

17. Mahmoud Darwish, "Mural," in *Unfortunately, It Was Paradise: Selected Poems*, trans. Munir Akash, Carolyn Forché, Sinan Antoon, Amira El-Zein, et al. (University of California Press, 2013), 151.
18. Bertolt Brecht, "To Those Born After," in *The Collected Poems of Bertolt Brecht*, trans. and ed. Tom Kuhn and David Constantine (W.W. Norton, 1923), 734–36.
19. Antonio R. Damasio, *Descartes' Error: Emotion, Reason and the Human Brain* (G.P. Putnam, 1994), 266.
20. Berger, *Here Is Where We Meet*, 161.
21. Song Dong, "Doing Nothing Garden, 2010–12," *dOCUMENTA (13)*, http://d13.documenta.de/research/research/view/doing-nothing-garden-2010-12/ and https://aaa.org.hk/en/collections/search/library/n084-song-dong-doing-nothing.
22. Cees Nooteboom, *All Souls' Day*, trans. Susan Massoty (Harcourt, 2001), 134–35.
23. Mahmoud Darwish, *I Don't Want This Poem to End: Early and Late Poems*, trans. Mohammad Shaheen (Interlink Books, 2017) ["An Interview with Mahmoud Darwish," 231–33]
24. Darwish, "Mural," 122.
25. Darwish, "Mural," 119.
26. Darwish, "Mural," 120.
27. Darwish, "Mural," 132.
28. Darwish, "Mural," 130.
29. Darwish, "Mural," 122.
30. Darwish, "Mural," 121.
31. Darwish, "Mural," 130.
32. Rawi Hage, *Stray Dogs* (Knopf Canada, 2022), 194.
33. Darwish, "Mural," 125.
34. "Silent poetry and sounding painting" is a term often used to describe the overlapping art forms of Chinese painting, poetry and calligraphy, 無聲詩有聲畫 wúshēng shī yǒushēng huà.
35. Darwish, "Mural," 120.

36. Wafa' Saleh, *The Translation of Poetic Form from Arabic to English: Mahmoud Darwish's "Mural" as a Case Study* (Master's thesis, An-Najah National University, Nablus, Palestine, 2021), 31, https://repository.najah.edu/items/11a14ec7-c685-443e-b3e8-345c2d62239c/full. I am indebted to Saleh's moving thesis, without which I would not have known that these lines do not appear in the translation by Munir Akash and Carolyn Forché.
37. Darwish, "Mural," 63–64.
38. Mahmoud Darwish, *In the Presence of Absence*, trans. Sinan Antoon (Archipelago Books, 2011), 15.
39. Some months after writing this essay I came across Fady Joudah's 2009 translation of *Mural*. I was startled and disconsolate to realize I had not known of this publication, even though I have loved Fady Joudah's poetry for years. His is a beautiful translation. In a footnote, he writes, "*Meem, Hā, Wāw, Dal* are the twenty-fourth, sixth, twenty-seventh, and eighth letters of the Arabic alphabet and make up the poet's name. In the Arabic text all the words listed after each letter are alliterations (to say the least) of that letter; this effect is impossible to duplicate in translation." Joudah conveys those eleven lines as follows:

    Meem / the infatuated, the orphaned, the finale of what has passed.
    Hā / the garden and the beloved, two puzzles and two laments.
    Meem / the adventurer, the readied and ready for his death, the one promised exile, and desire's ill patient.
    Wāw / farewell, the middle rose, loyal to birth wherever possible, and the pledge of parents.
    Dal / the guide, the road, the tear of a meadow that has perished, and a house sparrow that spoils me and bleeds me . . .

    Mahmoud Darwish, *If I Were Another: Poems*, trans. Fady Joudah (Farrar, Straus and Giroux, 2009), 144.

40. "Help me bear the brunt of my endurance." Darwish, "Mural," 140.
41. Darwish, "Mural," 119.
42. Darwish, "Mural," 123.
43. Darwish, "Mural," 171.
44. Julian Borger, "'We Took the Gloves Off': Ex-IDF Chief Confirms Gaza Casualties Over 200,000," *Guardian*, September 12, 2025, https://www.theguardian.com/world/2025/sep/12/israeli-ex-commander-confirms-palestinian-casualties-are-more-than-200000.

    A month earlier, Israeli general Aharon Haliva told Israel's Channel 12 TV station, "The fact that there are already 50,000 dead in Gaza is necessary and required for future generations. For everything that happened on October 7th, for every person on October 7, 50 Palestinians must die. It doesn't matter now if they are children." Emma Graham-Harrison, "Ex-Israeli Intelligence Chief Said 50 Palestinians Must Die for Every 7 October Victim," *Guardian*, August 17, 2025, https://www.theguardian.com/world/2025/aug/17/israeli-general-aharon-haliva-palestinians-7-october-gaza.
45. John Berger, "Al Rabweb," in Mahmoud Darwish, *Mural*, trans. Rema Hammami and John Berger (Verso, 2017), 4.
46. Omar El Akkad, *One Day, Everyone Will Have Always Been Against This* (Knopf, 2025), 107.
47. Mahmoud Darwish, "Palestine as Metaphor," as quoted by Munir Akash and Carolyn Forché in their introduction to *Unfortunately, It Was Paradise*.
48. Muhammad al-Zaqzouq, "Burning Books in Gaza," *Berlin Review*, Issue No. 8, January 2025, https://blnreview.de/en/ausgaben/2024-12/al-zaqzooq-burning-books-in-gaza-mud-ovens. Also published as "Hunger," *Paris Review*, October 3, 2025, https://www.theparisreview.org/blog/2025/10/03/hunger/. I understand that this unforgettable work will be part of al-Zaqzouq's forthcoming memoir.

The Red Record

IMMANUEL WILKINS

NOTES

1. Quoted in Valerie Wilmer, *As Serious as Your Life: Black Music and the Free Jazz Revolution, 1957–1977* (Serpent's Tail, 1992).
2. Frederick Douglass, *Narrative of the Life of Frederick Douglass, an American Slave*, ed. Houston A. Baker Jr. (Penguin Classics, 2018).
3. Interviewed in Arthur Taylor, *Notes and Tones: Musician-to-Musician Interviews* (Da Capo Press, 1996).
4. Saidiya Hartman, *Lose Your Mother: A Journey Along the Atlantic Slave Route* (Farrar, Straus and Giroux, 2007).
5. Fred Moten, *In the Break: The Aesthetics of the Black Radical Tradition* (University of Minnesota Press, 2003).
6. Avery F. Gordon, *Ghostly Matters: Haunting and the Sociological Imagination* (University of Minnesota Press, 2008).
7. Moten, *In the Break*.
8. Sylvia Wynter, "Unsettling the Coloniality of Being/Power/Truth/Freedom," *CR: The New Centennial Review* 3, no. 3 (2003).
9. George E. Lewis, *A Power Stronger Than Itself: The AACM and American Experimental Music* (University of Chicago Press, 2008).
10. Tina M. Campt, *Listening to Images* (Duke University Press, 2017).

Closing Remarks

OLA MOHAMMED

NOTES

1. Dan Hosken, *An Introduction to Music Technology* (Routledge, 2010).
2. Édouard Glissant, *Poetics of Relation* (University of Michigan Press, 2010), 27.
3. Julian Henriques, *Sonic Bodies: Reggae Sound Systems, Performance Techniques and Ways of Knowing* (Continuum International Publishing Group, 2011), xxi.

4. Ola Mohammed, "Haneen and Mohamed's Wedding," audio recording, personal collection, July 27, 2023; Europe Palestine Network, "Free Sudan!," Instagram post, @europe.palestine.network, March 26, 2025.
5. Frantz Fanon, *The Wretched of the Earth*, trans. R. Philcox (Grove Press, 1968 [original work, 1961]), 102–3.
6. Trinbagoforpalestine, "Grenada saying NO to the U.S. request to install military equipment in Maurice Bishop airport!," Instagram post, @trinbagoforpalestine, October 24, 2025; Matriarchal Circle, "Christie Residential School demolition ceremony," Instagram post, @matriarchalcircle, October 17, 2025.
7. Michel-Rolph Trouillot, *Silencing the Past: Power and the Production of History* (Beacon Press, 2015).
8. Rasheedah Phillips, *Dismantling the Master's Clock: On Race, Space, and Time* (AK Press, 2025), 15.
9. Bianca Beauchemin, *Arousing Freedoms: Re-Imagining the Haitian Revolution Through Sensuous Marronage* (Unpublished doctoral diss., University of California, Los Angeles, 2021), 6.
10. Fanon, *The Wretched of the Earth*, 38.
11. Christina Sharpe, *In the Wake: On Blackness and Being* (Duke University Press, 2016).
12. Aaron Joseph, *The Mariner Hospitality of The Quiet Storm: Pan-Africanism Without the Nation-State* (unpublished manuscript, 2025), 6.
13. Mahmoud Darwish, "Mural," in *Unfortunately, It Was Paradise: Selected Poems*, trans. Munir Akash, Carolyn Forché, Sinan Antoon, Amira El-Zein, et al. (University of California Press, 2013).
14. D'Angelo, "Send It On," *Voodoo* (Virgin Records, 2000).
15. Alice Vyvan-Jones, "The 'Voodoo' That Changed Everything: D'Angelo's Enduring Blueprint," *Earmilk*, October 26, 2025, https://earmilk.com/2025/10/26/the-voodoo-that-changed-everything-dangelos-enduring-blueprint/.

ABOUT THE ALCHEMISTS

GLEN SEAN COULTHARD is Yellowknives Dene, and an Associate Professor in the First Nations and Indigenous Studies Program, as well as the Departments of Political Science, at the University of British Columbia. He is the author of *Red Skin, White Masks: Rejecting the Colonial Politics of Recognition* (University of Minnesota Press, 2014), which won the Caribbean Philosophical Association's Frantz Fanon Award for Outstanding Book, the Canadian Political Science Association's CB Macpherson Award for Best Book in Political Theory and the Rik Davidson Studies in Political Economy Award for Best Book. He is also a co-founder of Dechinta Centre for Research and Learning, a decolonial, Indigenous land–based post-secondary program operating on his traditional territories in Denendeh (Northwest Territories).

CANISIA LUBRIN is a poet, prose writer and editor whose work explores ideas of social justice and the limits and possibilities of art, form and language. She is the award-winning author of three poetry collections: *Voodoo Hypothesis*; *The Dyzgraphxst*, which won the Griffin Poetry Prize and was a finalist for the Governor General's Literary Award; and *The World After Rain*. Her book of fiction, *Code Noir*, won the Carol Shields Prize for Fiction and was a finalist for the Governor General's Literary Award. Other honors include the Windham-Campbell Prize, the OCM Bocas Prize for Caribbean Literature, the Derek Walcott Prize and the Danuta Gleed Literary Award. Lubrin is the Poetry Editor at McClelland & Stewart, and coordinator of the University of Guelph Creative Writing MFA. She is well-known for her collaborations with other writers and artists, including in *Code Noir*, which contains fifty-nine drawings by celebrated visual artist Torkwase Dyson.

MADELEINE THIEN is the author of a story collection, *Simple Recipes*, and four novels: *Certainty*, *Dogs at the Perimeter*, *Do Not Say We Have Nothing* and *The Book of Records*. *Do Not Say We Have Nothing* was shortlisted for the Booker Prize, the Women's Prize for Fiction and the Folio Prize, and won the Governor General's Literary Award for Fiction, among other honors. *The Book of Records* was chosen as one of Barack Obama's "Favorite Books of the Summer," and won the Quebec Writers' Federation Paragraphe Hugh MacLennan Prize. It was longlisted for the National Book Critics Circle Award, shortlisted for the Climate Fiction Prize, and named a best book of the year by the *Globe and Mail*, the

New Yorker and the *Guardian*, among other accolades. Her books have been translated into twenty-five languages, and her stories and essays have appeared in the *New Yorker*, *Granta*, *Times Literary Supplement*, the *New York Review of Books* and elsewhere. As a librettest, she created *Chinatown*, a full-length opera by Alice Ping Yee Ho and Paul Yee. She was a Cullman Fellow at the New York Public Library, and in 2024 received the Engel Findley Award from the Writers' Trust of Canada. Born in Vancouver, Madeleine lives in Montreal.

Saxophonist, composer and educator **IMMANUEL WILKINS** burst onto the musical scene with his Blue Note debut, *Omega*, which was named the best jazz release of 2020 by the *New York Times*. Constantly seeking out creative connections within and outside the world of Jazz, Wilkins has worked with filmmakers Cauleen Smith and Ja'Tovia Gary; the sculptor Kennedy Yanko; the painter Leslie Hewitt; and the interdisciplinary artist Theaster Gates. In 2022, Wilkins released his sophomore album on Blue Note, *The 7th Hand*, which topped numerous year-end lists. In 2023, he was awarded three Downbeat Critics Poll Awards, including Best Alto Saxophonist, and in 2024 his quartet won the prize for best international live act by the Deutscher Jazzpreis. In 2024, Wilkins released his third and arguably his most adventurous recording to date: *Blues Blood*, co-produced by Meshell Ndegeocello. It was nominated for best international recording of the year by the Deutscher Jazzpreis and the Edison Jazz in the Netherlands. Immanuel was also named by *Jazz News* and *Jazz Magazine* as the best international jazz musician of the year.

OLA MOHAMMED is an assistant professor and York Research Chair Tier II in Black Sonic Cultures in the Humanities Department at York University. Her research focuses on Black Studies, Sound Studies, and Diaspora Studies. She specializes in interdisciplinary work exploring Black cultural production, social life, and being as sites of possibility.

CHRISTINA SHARPE is a writer, professor and Tier 1 Canada Research Chair in Black Studies in the Humanities at York University in Toronto. Sharpe is the author of *Monstrous Intimacies: Making Post-Slavery Subjects* (2010), *In the Wake: On Blackness and Being* (2016) and *Ordinary Notes* (2023), winner of the Hilary Weston Writers' Trust Prize for Nonfiction and the Hodler Prize, and finalist for the National Book Award for Nonfiction, the National Book Critics Circle Award for Nonfiction, the Los Angeles Times Book Prize for Current Interest and the James Tait Black Prize in Biography. In April 2024, she was awarded a Windham-Campbell Prize in Nonfiction and was named a Guggenheim Fellow. In May she received the Canada Council for the Arts Molson Prize for the Sciences and Humanities. Sharpe is currently working on *What Could a Vessel Be?* (FSG / Knopf Canada) and *Black. Still. Life.* (Duke University Press). Her writing has appeared in many artist catalogues and journals, including *Frieze*, *Paris Review*, *Harper's*, *BOMB Magazine* and *The Funambulist*.

ACKNOWLEDGEMENTS

For their support, intellectual and material, without which this Lecture could not have happened, we thank the following people, groups and organizations:

At York University: the Office of the President; the Office of the Dean of the Faculty of Liberal Arts and Professional Studies, and interim Dean Kathryn McPherson; the Department of Humanities, including the Graduate Program in Humanities and the Black Canadian Studies Certificate; Robarts Centre for Canadian Studies; the Canada Research Chair in Black Studies in the Humanities; Eve Haque and the York Research Chair in Linguistic Diversity & Community Vitality; Ola Mohammed, Assistant Professor and York Research Chair in Black Sonic Cultures; Carl James and the Jean Augustine Chair in Education, Community and Diaspora; the Graduate Program in Social & Political Thought; Ravi de Costa, Associate Dean, Research and Graduate Studies in the Faculty of Liberal Arts & Professional Studies.

Dionne Brand.

Canisia Lubrin.

Two of the first alchemists, who continue to support this work: Rinaldo Walcott, Carl V. Granger Endowed Chair, University of Buffalo; and Natalie Diaz, Founder and Director, Center for Imagination in the Borderlands, Arizona State University.

Andrea Davis, Professor and Associate Vice President EDI, Wilfrid Laurier University.

Leslie Sanders, University Professor Emerita, York University.

Grace Ngugi and Madina Agénor.

David Chariandy, Avie Bennett Chair of Canadian Literature, Department of English, University of Toronto; SA Smythe, Associate Professor and the Collaboratory for Black Poiēsis, University of Toronto.

The Butterfield Family Foundation.

The International Institute for Critical Studies in Improvisation at the University of Guelph.

For their unparalleled organizational skills, Jan Anderson, Assistant Professor of English, Trent University; Sheba Wiafe, PhD Student, Social and Political Thought, York University.

Department of English, Trent University.

Everyone at Penguin Random House Canada: Kristin Cochrane, CEO; Martha Kanya-Forstner, Publisher of Knopf Canada; Lynn Henry, Editor-in-Chief of Knopf Canada and Publishing Director, Alchemy by Knopf; Dionne Brand, Editorial Director, Alchemy by Knopf; Ashley Dunn, Associate Publisher, Knopf Canada.

Thank you to the York University Tech Staff, AV Services, and Communications and Publicity, especially Nathalia Whittingham and Nazrin Vakilova of Events and Internal Communications; the ASL interpreters; and the York University Book Store.

Above all, we wish to thank again the Lecturers for the extraordinary ways in which they thought together, on stage and in the pages of this book.